REVIEWERS AGREE

Steele is hardheadedly practical. He's worked out as sure-fire a method as you'll find for bridging the sexual-generation gap. *Michael Perkins, Screw Magazine*

Steele pulls no punches as he explains how to attract the young, from dress codes to actions. The honest approaches and advice are unusually solid and explicit. Everything from sex and the young woman to analyses of her value system and psyche with step-by-step courting scenarios, placing emphasis on strategy based on understanding. Men interested in a no-holds-barred approach will find this one of the most refreshing guides available. Women not involved in defining chauvinist behavior will learn a lot, too. *Diane Donovan, Chicago Tribune*

Gloves off truth! Far more than a dating book. Bold, harsh, funny, human, an unpredictable page-turner. A must read for divorced men. *Edward Haldeman, Single Fathers United*

Steele's unique style is nearly conversational, one of his strongest points as a writer. It makes for easy reading and creates and atmosphere totally lacking of preaching. His method of illustrating key points by telling actual stories of his own missteps and his successes makes for an interesting and engaging way to learn. *John F. Dempsey, Divorced Men's Council, ^*

Solid advice presentec   nes
hilarious, sometimes to   ok!
Kirk Matthews, Denver Si

Other books for men give pep talks and sure-fire opening lines. Steele cuts through that crap. His methods of setting up cross-routines with young women you are interested in will work with women of any age. Just this detailed advice is worth the price of the book. *Ron Macdonald, Single Scene, USA's largest singles newspaper*

How To
DATE
YOUNG
WOMEN
For Men Over 35

To:

Carla Ann

The young woman who taught me the most,
the hard way.

Thanks for the memories.

"There are no answers, only lessons."

Sue Tsunoda-Carroll
January 1987

ACKNOWLEDGMENTS

Every book begins with a concept but it takes conviction to turn that idea into the printed word. I'd like to thank Barbara Kristen for having confidence in me to do just that. It all began with her support and belief.

Once writing begins, it takes tenacity, discipline and sacrifice. For your understanding and enduring my sacrifice, Linda, Penny, Sue, Suzan, Syndee and Vanessa, my sincere appreciation.

Three years later, someone has to critique it. To every friend-reviewer, thanks for helping me see the forest not the trees, as well as for the vindication and encouragement.

Special thanks to John Raphael, truly a "big picture" editor, Gene Bellevue notable grammarian and diplomatic quality controller, and Syndee White, proofreader extraordinaire.

CONTENTS

"Deep in December,
it's nice to remember."

Bellafonte

What's It All About?

When you're 75 years old, what will give you pleasure?

My pleasure will probably come only from remembering. Thirty years from now, this is how it will happen.

There I am, dozing in my wheel chair. Somebody nudges me awake. I open my eyes and see giant tits straining the zippered front of a white uniform. I look up into the smiling black face of Mandy, the 20 year old attendant. She grins a toothy smile, "Time fo' sum sunshin', Donny." I nod politely, then drop my eyes to her large bosom and stare. Something's familiar. I struggle to remember.

She pushes me down the hall toward the veranda of the Golden Years Retirement Villa, pleasantly chattering away. As she talks, her dialect triggers my fogged up memory. Gradually old images, smells, feelings, sounds, sensations percolate up, flood my consciousness. I grin, start slobbering. In my mind, there I am again with my only black young lover, Genette. It's not 2016 any longer, it's 1979.

I have her bra off but I can't get these tight jeans down over her wonderfully big, 22 year old hips. To tease me she puts on her best jive talk, "Shit! You white boys don' kno' nuffin 'bout black ass," grabs the waist and peels them off, giggling the whole time.

I'm eating her. She takes my fingers off her nipples, and without a word, shows me I'm supposed to smash those giant tits against her chest, rub them 'round and 'round. She comes hard. Seconds later she comes harder. I get on and get us off, "bof us."

Thirty years from now what will you remember?

WHO'S READING THIS BOOK?

When Hugh Hefner first asked Barbi Benton out she said, "Well, I've, uh, never dated anyone over 23 before." Hef responded without hesitation, "That's okay. Neither have I."

You don't have Hefner's resources or knowledge. (Understated, right?) You're 40 plus or minus a few, divorced or about to be. You don't want to buy a young woman with gifts.

Some of you are experiencing the roller coaster emotions immediately following divorce or are acting out Middle Age Crazy. If that's you, these conditions have to be dealt with and resolved before attempting to practice what I preach. While getting it together, or at least into a pile, prepare yourself. Believe me, there's plenty to do and learn.

If you insist on going after young women before you're done with the emotional aftermath of a marriage ending, you'll set yourself back a year, that's if you have a giant ego and the skin of a rhino. Otherwise you'll get so humiliated you'll be happy to keep dating that 38 year old divorcee with three kids.

Finally, you're interested in, no, that's way too weak. You're lusting after young females. Trouble is, you don't have the slightest idea how to meet, talk with and date them.

WHAT YOU'RE ABOUT TO LEARN

Seen many men dating girls 18 to 24 years old? That's not because the men don't want to, now is it? Could it be ten million of them read the book quoted below? The poor saps think all they have to do is walk up and spew one of the author's "100 Best Opening Lines."

"The first, and really the only thing it takes to pick up girls, is to talk to them. Basically that's it. You find a chick who turns you on, you stroll right up to her, and you say, 'That dimple on your left knee is absolutely

sensational!' . . . That's all there is to it. If you can do
that, you can really pick up girls. By the truckloads!"

Eric Weber, author, *How To Pick Up Girls,* featuring
interviews with 25 beautiful girls.

Do you suppose Weber really believes the only thing
it takes "is to talk to them?" Maybe the 25 beautiful
girls he interviewed were in his wet dreams? The
"dimple" line and his others might work if a Tom
Selleck look-alike "strolled right up" and tried one.
That's assuming the "chick" could keep from laughing
hysterically, an assumption few men with three-digit
IQ's would make.

This is not a book of interviews with young women
and a writer's disguised guess as to what it all means.
This is a how-to book by a 46 year old man who has
done it for the past ten years and continues to do it.

I explain how to make your fantasies come true but
right now that's exactly what they are, fantasies. You
are going to learn how white, or raised white, middle
class young women think, what's important to them
and what they want from a man. You'll know what
you have to be and look like to attract her. I explain
where to find her, how to meet her, what to say to
her, principles of courting when you're 20 years older
than she is, what her real motives are for dating you,
how to behave on dates and how to seduce her. I tell
you the must do's as well as the no no's.

You're going to know what she has to offer and
what you absolutely cannot expect from her. You will
end up knowing what it really takes for a fortyish
man to date a twentyish woman. My experiences are
here for you to learn from, good ones, funny ones
and horror stories. When done reading you'll avoid
many of the mistakes I made as you learn the complex, delicate rituals and courtship practices insisted
upon by a young woman interested in an older man.

But you have to learn by doing. If you want to
break, then ride a horse, a wild young mare, you
can't read a book then sit on the corral fence theor-
izing about it. You have climb on and get thrown,

again and again. Eventually you'll realize you must talk gently to her, letting her know you intend no harm, showing no fear while radiating, "I'm in charge here." When you can do that she'll let you mount her and won't buck you off.

There are 13 million young women out there. At this very moment a half a million of them are being courted by men twice their age. Tens of thousands are having affairs with an older man right now, loving every minute. So how do you get involved?

You already date women, right? No matter how old she is the steps are the same: find-meet-talk-date. What's the problem then, you ask?

THE PROBLEM. Clearly stated, you don't know how to: (1) find her (2) meet her and (3) talk with her. Dating follows naturally if you converse with her correctly, based on the rules of engagement as she understands them. Presently you solve this three-part problem several times each year, the only difference is the female's age.

Find Her. Where do you find women right now? At work, in bars, attending classes, through friends, at parties and sometimes in the most unexpected places, like the post office. You find young women in the same places! No shit, you say. Well, everywhere except bars. Forget them, much more later.

My point is, finding her is not a big part of this problem. You have the primary resource to solve it sitting on top of your neck, your big head, not to be confused with your little head, which often prevents a solution to any part of this problem.

Meet Her. It's no different from meeting a woman. You introduce yourself, someone introduces you or she introduces herself. You have nearly all the skills and resources right now. This part of the problem is solved with only your big head, some chutzpah and learning a few techniques. But that's after, only after, you understand her, what she wants from you and what she's afraid of.

Talk With Her. Look closely at this one. It is made up of two tasks. Task A is delivering an opening line that won't make her laugh at you or scare her away. For Christ's sake, don't use any from *How to Pick Up Girls*, okay? Task B is sustaining the conversation long enough for her to realize you are (a) safe (b) interesting and (c) attractive.

ESSENCE OF THE PROBLEM. The substance, the essential difference, the core, or, to put it more succinctly, the entire goddamned thing comes down to Task B with its four sub-tasks.

Sustained Contact. You have to talk with her for a minimum of four or five minutes. At this point you don't know much about talking with anyone under 25. You don't yet have the ability to carry on a conversation she can, like, relate to. You know, like, on her level. Simple, you know, like friendly, relaxed, you know, like, well, totally casual. No, they're not all air heads or valley girls. But "casual" is what every last one of them needs to realize you're not dangerous. She is afraid you might be physically dangerous as well as socially and emotionally dangerous.

Physical Danger. She thinks you could be the Night Stalker's brother or a dirty old man trying to cop a feel. Being relaxed and friendly makes it possible for her to see you're safe. You do this with women. Young women just take longer.

But it isn't how much longer it takes her. The real problem is your lust, your excitement, your impatience, your lack of confidence, your fear of rejection. These combine, causing you to radiate bad vibrations. She picks them up and thinks you could be very dangerous, at which point she says, "Later, old man," with or without words.

Social Danger. You'll soon learn how to control yourself and your emotions when talking with her. Then you must figure out how to calm her fear of the threat you pose to her socially. In simple English, you learn how to not be direct or obvious. You have to be casual enough so she doesn't have to worry her friends, peers, and possibly her boyfriend, will ridicule or reject her if she's seen talking with you.

The problem is not her fear, it's you but not your

emotions. You haven't mastered the art of being casual. It is not necessary, often counterproductive, to use a slow easy approach with women. If you aren't casual when talking with a woman in front of her friends, she's not worried, "He was trying to pick me up. So what?"

A young woman's not only worried about being seen talking with you. She has far more to lose by dating you. If her friends find out she will be ostracized. No young man in her circles will consider her as a wife, feeling she is used merchandise, some old man's cast off. The way our world works people only smirk about you but they strongly condemn her, calling her sick, a gold digger, promiscuous or a slut. With patience, her view of you as socially dangerous can be transformed into the realization you are discreet, subtle and sensitive to her situation.

Emotional Danger. She thinks you're so powerful, so knowledgeable, you will be able to sexually use her, then discard her. This is her biggest fear. Although this sounds impossible to overcome, it isn't. I spend fewer pages on this than the others. Trial and error, mostly error, will teach you what to do.

INTERESTING AND ATTRACTING HER. I don't mean to be glib but after you know how to deal with her fears you only have to be yourself. Of course you have to look like someone she'd like to talk with but that's all explained. Then you have to religiously follow the *Ten Commandments Of Meeting* and the *Eleven Commandments Of Courtship*. You must also have "Answers To Inevitable Questions" down pat. At that point you only have to get up, dust yourself off and get back on every time you get thrown. Like Paul Hornung said, "Practice, practice, practice."

THE PROBLEM CLEARLY RESTATED. She's afraid and you don't know how to put her at ease. There it is in one simple sentence. Some elaboration. The only difference between finding, meeting, talking with and dating a 37 year old and a 20 year old, is learning how to calm and neutralize the younger woman's far more intense fear of the consequences. To do that, you must *Understand Her.*

Understand Her

I describe the unsettled life and troubled times of the typical 20 year old who can become interested in dating an older man. When you understand her you only need to know, on average, younger ones are worse in every way, better in none. The older ones are better in every way, worse in none.

Double the general disarray of this 20 year old's life for a 19 year old. Quadruple it for an 18 year old. If she's still in high school, multiply by ten.

For each year past 21 her problem is reduced by twenty five percent. A 23 year old living away from home has eliminated two thirds of the 20 year old's negative situation, if she has no kids. With even one, her problems are twenty times greater than any 18 year old's.

A couple of years out of high school her old world falls apart. Friends move away or marry and have kids, others stay at college all year. She's standing with one foot in the teen age world, the other in the adult world, at 20.

However, a female of 22 retains all the good qualities of being young but has discarded most of the baggage and burdens of youth. With her enlarged sense of self she's much simpler to deal with, requiring far less time and energy on your part initially and throughout the affair. But, I had to find out for myself about 18 year olds. You will too, probably.

THE TYPICAL 20 YEAR OLD

She lives with a couple of roommates but only recently left home. She's never lived with her boyfriend. She has a job or is going to college. She has a car. She doesn't have a drug problem. She may have had an abortion, the odds are 80-20 against it. Her IQ is 110. She gave her first hand job at 15, then gave up her virginity at the Junior Prom. Her best sex was with some guy she picked up one weekend in Palm Springs. He was 26 but never called when she got back to LA like he promised.

She smokes marijuana or snorts coke at parties and at home when she's bored. She drinks at home, at parties and in clubs and bars where she sees herself as a grown up. She's not shy but not a rowdy extrovert either. She follows fashion but isn't a trendy person. She's had the same boyfriend for a year and a half. At 23, he still lives with his parents and has a job, sometimes.

To really understand her, get your fogged up memory working. Think back 20 years. What was it like being powerless? What was it like to only have a few dollars? What was it like thinking everyone was watching you? What was it like not knowing what you were doing, having to bullshit your way through? Remember what an asshole you were at 20. Recall how totally cool you pretended to be, acting like you knew all about life and love. She's no different.

CONFLICT AND CONFUSION - SITUATION NORMAL. She's internalized most values our culture sanctimoniously preaches but she's beginning to notice widespread hypocrisy. She is questioning the rationality of some ideas and is considering the possibility that many rules for behavior are wrong, not just for her, but for all society.

Strong, conflicting emotions generated by her own mutually exclusive values and goals cause her moods to come and go without warning. She often feels out of control and compensates for it by believing in something, anything. In short, a self-contradicting blend of Jerry Falwell's, Ann Landers' and Helen

Gurly Brown's rules and regulations.

She's trying to become the woman she has tacked up on the wall inside her head. Comparing herself to that ideal everyday, she finds herself lacking. She is confused about life, love, sex, marriage, babies, career, parents, boyfriends, lovers and on and on. Her life is a jumble. Unsettled about the future, she decides "once and for all" at least twice a month. She's insecure because of her lack of knowledge, experience, power, money and independence. When comparing herself to other young women, she sees only their facades of self confidence. Having no idea her friends are just as uncertain, she feels isolated, alone. The more insecure she is, the more she covers it up. She appears aloof, cool and sophisticated, especially to you.

Thoughts and feelings arise from nowhere. She wants to stab her Dad and choke her 13 year old sister because the brat gets to do everything she was forbidden at that age. She feels "sick" for wanting to feel her co-worker's big tits. Guilt arises when announcing she doesn't go to church any more. After masturbating she wonders if God was really watching. Sometimes she's so terribly lonely she seriously considers killing herself. To her there's no reason for these feelings. Her problems seem monumental. She has no idea it's normal, late adolescent dues paying. She has no perspective from which to judge.

For months she knows what she is and what she wants, then suddenly she has a change of heart. No longer does she want to be a Cosmo Girl, she wants to be a trendy teenager again. Six weeks later she changes her image to Yuppie In Training. After working in an office for a half a year she realizes how hard it is to make money. Then she goes to a romantic movie with Jimmy. They talk about getting married. She decides she'd like to stay at home, an ivy covered cottage, and raise two cute kids.

She believes that if she does the right things, eventually she'll be rewarded. To her there's only one right way to do anything, including having a relationship with a male. You're a male. Prepare yourself.

"It will be easy when I'm 25," is one of her deeply held beliefs. She thinks she'll be able to cope effectively with "men," parents and life in general. All young people think everything's supposed to go smoothly. They have no idea life is nothing but a series of obstacles, feeling God or fate is punishing or testing them when a problem comes into their lives.

When she meets a male in society's acceptable age range she sees only a potential husband. She and her counterparts believe in the nuclear family and want to be the center of one someday. The difference is, in her family everyone will be happy. She thinks she can make it work, just as you and I did.

Don't argue or try to convince her she's wrong about this belief or any others. Only offer your views if pressed severely. It is not useful to debate with her. Life, and you're part of life, will eventually prove how ridiculous and hypocritical most of our culture's rules, traditions and gender-specific goals are.

The self concept she developed from six years old until she started her period is lurking in the background. Her new self is solidifying but it's in constant jeopardy as she confronts more and more of what the adult world has to offer, including you. Under stress she turns into a brat of eleven you'd love to strangle or a frightened five year old you have to hold on your lap.

She feels like a failure from her sophomore year of high school on, if she does not have a boyfriend. It doesn't mean she won't have an affair with you when she has one. It only means he ensures she won't have to stay home on Saturday night.

She wants to be independent but fears being alone. She was raised to be a virgin when she married but "does it" all the time with Jimmy. She dreams of being rich and famous. She enjoys pretending she's an adult but likes to be babied.

She and most of her friends, male and female, have whacked out parents: neurotic parents, dying parents, divorcing parents, Jesus freak parents, alcoholic parents, possessive parents, neglecting mothers or molesting fathers. She wants o-u-t, out. She hates her job, it's menial and boring. Her boss "teases" her about taking her on a "business" trip and keeps wanting to rub her back. Her friends are only fair in good weather. Debbie, her best friend, was kissing Jimmy at the party last week. But, she wants her friends to think she's cool. She wants to make lots of money, spend it on cool clothes, cool cars, cool travel, on being "totally" cool. She and her counterparts are superficial not because they are genuinely phony, the world's still a bit too big for them.

She is experimenting with life, testing herself to see how powerful she really is. At the same time she's searching for a stable identity, choosing and rechoosing, marriage or college, getting a job and moving out or staying at home and doing nothing.

It is a time of stress and pressure you have forgotten about. To her the stress and pressure are real even if, to you, it is lightweight solvable stuff.

When she meets you she suspects you're married and lying about being divorced. Don't press the point. She considers herself sophisticated for being suspicious.

She's still becoming the person she's going to be while you're trying to un-become the person you've been. You're trying to return to adolescence. She's leaving it behind.

YOU CAUSE EVEN MORE CONFUSION. Just yesterday afternoon she was lying in your arms contented as a puppy with a full tummy. Today, after a fender bender, the whole universe is falling apart.

She's confused by the flood of emotions you cause in her. During one week she feels elated, guilty, foolish, sexual, womanly, appreciated, accepted, curious, ignorant, naive, inept, silly, whorish, glamorous, sad, sensual, romantic, grown-up, lustful, horny, sated, terrified, brave, embarrassed, proud, shy, exhibitionistic, childlike, daughter-like and a hundred others you and I can't empathize with.

Carla and I were lying in bed after superb orgasmic sex that lasted for a half an hour. As the glow faded, she said in a tiny, painful voice, "A year ago I was a virgin! Things are not like they told me."

She thinks she must be in love, otherwise she wouldn't be having such grand sex with you. At the same time she thinks, often out loud, "What am I doing?" She's breaking all the rules and gets a charge out of doing just that. But, on her way home she feels like a cheap slut for sucking a 45 year old cock.

She's volatile, impulsive and irrational. Her confusion drives you crazy. She picks a fight so she can break up with you. She cancels a date and make sure you know on some level she's going out with a boy. She's young, confused, ignorant and scared. If your affair's been going for three months or more, add bored.

Sounds pretty negative, right? Well, my friend, I chose to tell you the bad news first. Why? Because if you think everything's going to be easy or you're not interested in taking the bad with the wonderful, you can put the book down now. Call up that 38 year old with three kids. Or, you can get back to important activities, like watching tv or hanging out in bars.

If you're serious about young women, keep reading and absorb the negatives. Digest them. Mull them over. They are key to understanding her, something you must do before you can ever hope to talk with her, let alone date her. In a few chapters, you'll get the good news.

THE 20 YEAR OLD'S AGENDA

She's primarily interested in getting a husband-to-be on the hook. (Much more later in *Boyfriends*.) It takes her a year of going steady to feel she's got him under control.

Once this is accomplished she wants to see what she's been missing. She goes dancing or to parties with "the girls" where she practices interacting with new boys and young men. After a few months she's ready. Her experimentation begins with another boy, her naive version of an affair.

She enjoys the excitement of getting away with something but then realizes he's only a boy just like Jimmy. She wants to try on a "man," so she finds one, Randy RedPorsche, a 28 year old singles' bar professional. He bangs her on Thursday nights when she's "out with the girls" and on Monday nights when Jimmy's "out with the boys."

When Jimmy finds out, he breaks up with her. But soon, RedPorsche gets bored and trashes her. She begs Jimmy to take her back. He does. Each claims to have discovered how much he really loves the other after only four weeks apart. They prove it by exchanging wedding vows. In reality they're both terrified of the single world, so they flee to the "safety" of marriage and a "dependable" partner.

If Jimmy won't take her back she tries a brief but uninspired crack at single life. After getting screwed literally and figuratively by one user after another, two things are possible. Either she becomes as plastic as the rest and starts hanging out in pickup bars. Or, if you're lucky, she drops out of the swinging singles' world and dates several young men she knew from high school or met at college as she searches for another husband-to-be.

If you meet her after the breakup you have a much better chance with her than before her first fling. If she's abandoned the bar scene your chances improve ten times. If she and her boyfriend are working on their relationship you're chances are a hundred times better. "Working on" means she's keeping her freedom to date or he is. They go out with each other only when lonely, bored or horny.

Back up a bit. Let's assume she wasn't going steady but was living with her boyfriend for a year.

At first she enjoys playing house and acting like a grown-up, at least what she fantasizes adults behave like. As time goes by it becomes apparent this is not as much fun as it should be but she does not discuss it with him, she only complains to her girl friends or her mother. The younger, the more she feels she's missing out on what her contemporaries are experiencing.

If she hasn't given up on her mini-marriage she tries to go out with the girls. He feels insecure and reacts according to his personality, machoing out and insisting she stay home or wimping out, acting like his whole world is ending. No matter which way he reacts she's so angry she feels free to cheat on him and does, with the first male of any age who treats her nice.

Her motive is to hurt him and get him to change, meaning she has to get caught. If Jimmy's too trusting or too dumb to not figure it out, she confesses in order to create the scene(s) necessary for Jimmy to change. You are paying attention, aren't you?

This couple struggles along until they get married or one of them meets somebody new, and leaves. If a primary motive for moving in with him was to escape neurotic parents, she will live with a couple of girl friends while she looks for a new husband-to-be.

These events are typical for those who don't marry within two years out of high school. She has this experience between 17 and 23, depending on her maturity, but for most it happens when she's 20, plus or minus a year.

WHAT SHE KNOWS ABOUT SEX

Mummy and Daddy pounded it into her young head boys are only interested in one thing. By the age of 20 she believes it. Every male to date has tried to pack her pipe within hours or on the second date. The exception is her boyfriend, he was "honorable" for at least for a month.

Her actual experience is mostly mediocre intercourse with possibly one good, not great, lover. Contrary to the media's exploitation, most young women engage in sexual relations only with fiances or steady boyfriends.

However, when she doesn't have a boyfriend, a likable, young enough to marry guy (22-29) dates her easily and gets in her pants quickly. He has a wide choice of young women and she knows it. Experience

has taught her to "get it on" or he won't be back,
then there'll be no chance to hook a potential husband. After ten or more of these encounters which
take place between boyfriends, she finally realizes
these young men are using her intense desire to
become Queen For A Day to get her on her back. At
that point she begins playing "The Dating Game" much
rougher with all males, including you. She's reached
23 or 24 by then.

The young men who precede you think eating pussy
is something one does only to get head in return.
They are not concerned with her pleasure or enjoyment except for Randy RedPorsche's younger brother,
Danny Manly. He wants her to believe he's super stud
so she'll rave about him to her girl friends. He hopes
word will get back to his buddies so they will think
he's a "real man." Other boys and young men, including her boyfriend, don't encourage her to take an
active part in any sexual activities except when they
want a blow job. She's only a notch on their guns.
But each and every time, she hoped to be loved.

In my experience only a few young women have
ever achieved orgasm as the result of a young partner's actions. And, with some of them, it was only an
accident, an unrepeatable accident. (Don't concern
yourself with this the first few times, as explained in
Sex With Her.) Most just give in to intercourse, and
although it's pleasurable, it's not like in the movies
or her trashy romance novels.

She believes sex is okay, it feels good but it's not
all that great. She can't understand what all the
excitement's about. After lying to her and manipulating her for weeks, he comes in 30 to 90 seconds. She
and her contemporaries just don't have any great
experiences they're trying to repeat.

Young women rarely need sex like their older
counterparts who've discovered, by about 28, that
priests and all other purveyors of anti-sex propaganda
were, and are, full of shit. Very seldom will you meet
a young woman who loves sex. Those who do began
early. They're rebellious, independent and have learn-

ed to take charge of their own orgasms. If she's had an older boyfriend who can sustain intercourse she finds it wonderful, fun and nourishing.

HER FIRST OLDER MAN. She heard about dirty old men as she was growing up. The tone of voice and disapproving faces made her fear older men. When she was 14, Mr. Pious, the Sunday school teacher, Mr. Boneher, the History Teacher, Dr. Feelit, her pediatrician, or even her own Uncle Dick, tried to fuck her. She didn't expect it. She trusted him. She thought it would be some stranger hiding in a dark alley. All this is in the back of her pretty head. Don't even talk like the man Mummy warned her about.

EXPERIENCE CAN HELP, BUT. Most limit themselves to young males, you know, marriable. That's why they're disappointed, unfulfilled and interested in you. An experienced 21 year old's idea of variety means a tall boy, a muscled boy, a black boy, a chubby boy and for a radical thrill, Randy RedPorsche's roomie, the 29 year old Sammy SilverBeemer.

Living with a boy does not help her all that much. It does get her over the mystery of sex, helps clear up unrealistic ideas she had about male plumbing and does away with old wives' tales.

Those who have lived with their boyfriends are sexually experienced to his level, meaning they have tried everything he knows. She doesn't get to learn how to really enjoy herself because he is so limited in his knowledge and ability. If she attempts to be assertive he's intimidated and manipulates her out of experimenting with anything except "swallowing it" or trying the "back door."

UNDERSTANDING ALL 18-24 YEAR OLDS

Young women, even girls as young a 14, have the same undesirable, unpleasant qualities of adult women, they are catty and viciously competitive over males. Don't be surprised if you have to contend with the 17 year old sister of your 21 year old lover vying for your attention and favors.

Although this sounds like it might be fun, it isn't.

It turns ugly quickly if either gets her ego bruised. One will threaten to tell dad or the other's boyfriend.

RANDOM THOUGHTS. The world feels new and fresh to the young. They sincerely feel it can be changed and they think they're the ones who can do it. Never be cynical or laugh at her idealism.

Young females need to be hugged and cuddled. When you get the chance give her plenty of both.

They are not comfortable with competition or competing except with each other for males. Don't stress winning when involved in any sport if she's around. Don't drive like it's Memorial Day at Indy. Don't play any games with her if you share the view of Al Davis of the Raiders, "Just Win, Baby." Don't let her win but don't take a backgammon game seriously.

Girls from the extreme upper and lower socio-economic levels experience intercourse younger. Nothing matters, they have too much or too little. I don't discuss them.

The girl who places high value on academic achievement is strikeout city. Her focus is in the wrong place to enjoy you while she's pleasing her parents or society with a high GPA.

None of them fuck like they dance. None of them fuck like they dress. They have no idea how overdone they are in these two areas.

Her soap operas, television programs and trash novels have convinced her "sugar" comes with the territory. She's not really a gold digger. She just thinks that's part of the deal. Squash this concept early on and I mean right away.

However, it is okay to be somewhat nice to her. Take her places Jimmy never would. Small, inexpensive, thoughtful gifts are appropriate. Bigger things come later, at the same time you'd give them to a woman you enjoyed dating for months and months.

When she begins reading *Cosmopolitan* your star shines far brighter. Buy her a subscription.

There is a period each year when you can count on a thin supply of young women, Election Day through

New Year's Day. Most grit their teeth and endure horrible treatment by their boyfriends or put off breaking up with a someone who bores them shitless. Their world will end, they feel, without "someone special" in their lives during the holidays.

Even worse, they get serious with anyone they're even casually dating in November to ensure they can share "the joy of Christmas." Watch out! This includes you. Tactfully keep your distance but send or give her a nice gift. Stay in contact. She'll recover from this culturally induced madness just in time for a truly important event, the Super Bowl.

GENERAL ADVICE. Lower your desire for physical beauty from 9.5 to 7.5 and watch fifty percent of the competition disappear. If you concentrate on 9.0 and above you'll be frustrated and humiliated most of the time. Stick with 6.5's to 8.0's. From my experience the young woman who is average looking with an average figure is easier to meet, a much nicer person, a better human being, as well as being more fun than any stunning looking one. She feels appreciated for the first time in her life. She is.

Forget the high schooler. Her head is up her ass and will be for two more years. Proms, football games, Friday dances, Jimmy's bitchin', totally rad, new Vee Dub convertible.

Forget the big titted girl. The competition is, pardon the pun, too stiff. Every male within 500 miles is interested. If you insist, never mention her figure and dare not look at those double D's.

Forget the beauty queen or any beauty. The competition is, pardon the same pun, too stiff. She's able to pick and choose and she's heard it all before from practiced experts. Too much trouble, thinks she really is a princess. Besides, you have to deal with the attention she attracts no matter where you go. People notice and remember you being with her. Not a great idea.

Forget the disco dolly. She's the one who spends two hours getting ready for work, three hours for the disco. Her $70 hair cut requires 90 minutes for curling and spraying. She wears the latest, most expensive clothes, usually $300 worth just to go dancing. She's concerned only with image, too insecure to be herself, while looking for a disco dick to impress and marry.

Forget all born agains, girls with doves, fish or "I Love Jesus" symbols on their cars or around their necks. They look normal. Some can even talk normal. Believe brother, believe. They're marching to the beat of a different drummer. Say Amen.

WHIM DRIVEN. The younger, the more ruled by instant gratification they are. For example, a 22 year old can agree to a trip to Palm Springs in two weeks and wait, then turn down a "better offer" three days before departure. A typical 19 year old has difficulty keeping a date to go night skiing at Big Bear three days from now. If girl friends call and want her to go to Vegas two hours before she's due at your place, she'll call and apologize, maybe.

As she spends more and more time with you the more realistic she becomes no matter how young she is. Just being around you has a tranquilizing effect on her. No longer is everything ruled hour by hour. In only a month she's thinking ahead two or three days at a time. Eventually she can plan from week to week. If you last long enough, from month to month. You'll never make it until she's able to think, plan and execute six months in advance.

As I'm writing this I'm planning a trip to Hawaii with a 19 year old. Our affair has been going for nine months. Recently she's learned it is possible to plan ahead. Two months into the relationship she was still so impulsive she ruined a three day weekend not being able to turn down a "better offer" at the last moment. We survived my ensuing explosion. I won't predict if it'll be Aloha or Adios in two more months.

TEDDY BEARS. The younger she is, the more suspect you are. Sometimes she drags along her Teddy Bear, a female friend, on the first pseudo date. Don't resent it. She has to take this initial step on her terms, not yours. Her friend serves several functions: body guard, validation of your attractiveness, support in case you overwhelm her, someone to talk with or get her out if you're boring.

Teddy comes along until your chosen feels safe with you. This includes day ski trips, beach excursions, a "spontaneous" dinner or anything else. Be enthusiastic about it. Include Teddy in all conversations and fun. Make friends with her. She will be grading you. Remember, she has the ear of your future lover and will certainly bend it.

It's not productive to flirt strongly with Teddy but let her know you find her pleasant and attractive as a female. If you patronize Teddy, you can shine it on, forever.

Anytime there are two females involved things get complicated quickly. Teddy, especially if she's more experienced, may have given herself the assignment of testing you under battle conditions. She'll bait you with emotionally loaded questions about sex or religion. Teddy may even bluntly ask how your children handled the divorce! If she's attracted to you she may resent her feelings and try to destroy you in front of her friend so neither can have you. Strange? Yes, but true.

If Teddy decides she wants you for herself she undermines everything you've built to date. In the end she will feel like shit for what she did and won't go out with you, either.

The younger she is, the more likely she'll bring Teddy along. I even had it happen with a 26 year old.

REBS AND OTHERS. They come in two basic models: conformists and rebels. Dependent, not independent, is what conformists are all about.

Rebs are outnumbered ten to one but what a great tenth. They aren't hard to spot. I can tell by her walk. They drive like maniacs, swear like sergeants, drink, smoke dope, snort coke and flaunt their bodies at me and other males of any age. For entertainment they intentionally piss off their parents or boyfriends. My kind of young women, the ones I'm strongly attracted to and enjoy getting emotionally attached to.

By being a rebel she defines herself as different from her parents, different from peers, different from adults of any kind. But, she's just different, having only found who and what she isn't.

LOOKIE LOU'S WILL SLEEP WITH YOU. Many have been interested in me only because they were curious. After a couple of dates they go to bed with me once or twice, then I never hear from them again. They found out what they wanted to know and decided, "It's not all that hot." Or they're so guilt ridden about Jimmy they can't continue.

The ones who didn't like me search for excitement with some other grown-up male. Those who feel guilty go back to "messin' around" with boys, somehow that's not bad. Or, they make up for the transgression with me by getting engaged and remain monogamous until a year after the honeymoon.

Relax, accept being a curiosity. Don't feel indignant. She's just looking. You're an experiment in her life. That's how she learns. Be glad you could help.

HER MOTIVES FOR DATING YOU

You're asking her to go against everything parents, boyfriend, church, society and girl friends have drilled into that pretty young head and heart of hers. Why will she do it?

One element of her motivation is the desire to be seriously fucked, the way she's heard it's supposed to be done. As you now know her best experience does not begin to measure up to what she's heard from other girls, read in *Cosmopolitan* or seen in the movies. And, "fer sure," there is the stereotype of older men as knowledgeable, experienced lovers.

She knows there must be more to it. But this is one of her darkest, most closely held secrets, slightly behind masturbating and feeling terribly lonely. She fantasizes what a "real man" would do with her. If she's a bit drunk she talks to her closest girl friend about what it should be like. Don't get this wrong. She's not obsessed with sex but wonders if she's missing something important.

So far her boyfriend's best efforts aren't much. He

wants his cock sucked all the time. He's reluctant to give her head and has no idea a clit isn't a miniature dick, if he even knows where it is. He lasts two minutes after entering her. She and her contemporaries know, on some level, there's more to it.

Part of the attraction is your age. It makes you different, plain and simple. You are attracted to her because she's different from 38 year old divorcees. (How's that for an understatement?) Also, your age qualifies you to participate with her in a forbidden romance, a turn on to females of any age.

She wants to experience life. You have the knowledge and money to show her a world she's only seen on television and read about in *People*. Older lovers have lots to offer says *Cosmopolitan*. One of her girl friend's acquaintances has one. She's ready to give it a try.

She may want to shame and degrade her parents. This girl plays a game called The Goy Ploy. She picks a male to infuriate and embarrass her parents: a goy if she's Jewish, or a Jew if her parents found Jesus. Others to piss off Mum and Dad: bikers, Mexicans, punks or an older man. Paying attention?

She has to get caught with you so she can make a giant scene(s) to rub her parent's noses in the whole sordid affair. That'll show them they were bad to her. Then they'll see it's their fault she turned out to be a bad girl.

Daughters of the rich sometimes are just bored and want to do something "totally radical." But, poor little rich girls play Goy Ploy, too. Be extra careful. Irate wealthy parents like to prove themselves blameless by threatening legal action or using their connections to punish you "for seducing our sweet, innocent baby girl."

FOOLISH ASSUMPTIONS. As a married man I was able to easily meet and "date" young women. After a few conversations and lunch she'd realize I only wanted to nail her to the mattress, then to the wall at the nearest motel.

After three of these "affairs" I realized it was not

necessary to beat around the bush, so to pun. I only had to be discreet and make it tactfully clear what I wanted. She simply chose to participate in some serious fucking or diplomatically passed. She knew from my approach and attitude that if she played "chase me, catch me, fuck me" I'd lose interest and she'd lose "fuck me." Courtship was simpler and faster then. No confusion about long term possibilities, the goal was straightforward.

My foolish assumption: after getting divorced I would be able to meet and have real dates with young women.

WRONG! Married men are toys, nothing to take seriously.

When she "dates" a married man she doesn't feel used. She knows what the score is. If she gets entangled she only blames herself because she reads Dear Abby every day.

Now that I'm single, she's confused about my purpose and goal. "He's kind of a potential husband but he's so old." Everything's muddled. She wants to get married someday but she's been used and lied to by every guy over 26 she's ever been out with. No matter what I say or do she thinks I am primarily interested in her slit.

I'm something she's not encountered before. I don't want to just nail her. I want to have a caring, romantic, fun-filled affair for as long as we enjoy each other. She knows that on some level from my attitude and approach, sometimes she even asks me directly.

"Gosh! An affair? Really? You know, like, I don' know. Jeez. What about my boyfriend?"

To answer that question and to really understand her, you have to be clear on why she almost always has a boyfriend. But first you need to know *Which Young Women*, otherwise, you'll waste time pursuing the wrong one.

"A seven, who will date you three times, is a ten."

The Author

Which Young Women

Let's divide the female population into Women, Almost Women, Young Women and Girls. Women are over thirty, 25 to 29 year olds are Almost Women, Young Women are 18 to 24, Girls are under 18.

Women break into four groups, each requiring a different courtship approach: 30-34, 35-39, 40-45 and over 45. Almost Women are courted as: Over 25 or Not 30. Young Women only cover seven years but there are four distinct courtship groups. Girls can be thought of as a fifth. The name of each group represents your task when trying to date a member:

> 21 to 24 - Hard
> 20 to 21 - Harder
> 19 to 20 - Hardest
> 18 to 19 - Impossible
> Jail Bait - Preposterous

THE TARGET POPULATION

White or raised white, 18 to 24. Healthy, non-handicapped. Upper lower class to lower upper class. Slightly below average to Playmate of the Month looks. Average to genius IQ's. Almost virgins to Rosy Roundheels. High school grads to Stanford PhD's. With and without boyfriends, divorced, living or lived together. Working, unemployed, under employed, students. Introverts or extroverts. Urban, suburban, small to mid-sized city dwellers. No car, bicycle, moped, daddy's car, own car. Living at home, in the dorm, has an apartment with roommate, own apartment. Beer drinkers to advanced free basers. In short, C minus and up.

WE'RE NOT INTERESTED IN THESE

Jail bait. Over 25. Ghetto dwellers. Low rider Mexicans. Most orientals. Lower and upper class. Virgins. Standoff Ugly. Stupid. Hookers. High school dropouts. Married, engaged or separated. Rural and small town residents. Druggies, biker chicks and all other lowlife's. In short, D plus and down.

WHAT A DIFFERENCE A YEAR MAKES

No individual young woman will fit the descriptions below. Every blue moon you will meet a 21 year old woman. That's woman, not young woman. At other times you'll find a 27 year old who is no more than a high school girl, an unemployed, college drop out, spoiled rotten princess, still living at home.

18-19. Working or in college, high school ways guide her life. Just testing herself and teasing you. Lives at home or in the dorm. Is dependent, not independent, even if she acts like it. Always has a boyfriend who bores her shitless but she's afraid to break up and be on her own. Very limited sexual experience. Sometimes uses no birth control. In general, a hassle. A tremendous amount of time and patience is required and seldom worth the effort. Brighter, extroverted ones might be worth a few weeks of courtship. Suzy, Betsy and Tina were. I rarely bother any more.

19-20. Has dropped many high school values and is beginning to realize there may be more to life than cruising the boulevard. Been to Palm Springs where she picked up a boy and "slept with him." If in college or working in a big office, she's considered "sleeping with" her prof or boss. Gets into bars and clubs with fake ID and feels really grown up there. More able to deal with life and it's problems but she's still moving in old circles. Coming alive sexually but it confuses her when she wants someone other than Jimmy. About 30 percent are on the pill, most others take precautions. Substantial time and effort required. May be worth it if you like her as a person.

When you are making progress she's worth two months of courtship but no more. Time's a' wastin'. Carla was worth it all. See the book's dedication page to find out why.

20-21. See "Typical 20 Year Old."

21-24. Delightful. Over their first love and reaching for the unknown. But can still behave like a 14 or 40 year old within an hour. 21-22, delightful, 22-23 delightful plus, 23-24 delightful, degrading into "wanna be married," 24-25, on the steep part of degrading but still far better than any woman.

HOME OR AWAY?

The one who doesn't live at home is always a better choice. She doesn't have the daily hassle of dealing with neurotic parents, envious sisters and protective brothers. With only Jimmy to snow, she can spend the night or go away with you on weekends.

I had an on again-off again, sometimes affair with Jean over a two year stretch and an affair of eight months with Tina. They both lived at home but were worth all the shenanigans required. I'd do it again with the right young woman.

COEDS OR WORKING GIRLS?

Coeds don't have much money, they have lots of time. Working girls don't have much time but unlike coeds, their world doesn't revolve around a lack of money.

A college girl is more educated, knows the nine planets but has little understanding of what really makes the world go 'round. She doesn't know much about men since her choice is limited to Joe College or dirty old professors. She's a quick study, having read about older lovers and smart enough to realize you could be one hell of a good time.

The working girl is pragmatic. She's in the real world, not the academic one. Since she's "out there among 'em" every day, she understands males of every age much better. She has a beginner's grasp of what makes the world work. Brighter ones are quick to realize the benefits of an older lover.

THE BEST YOUNG LOVER

The ideal young woman lives away from home, without a boyfriend, with smarts. A coed who works or a working girl going to college. She's serious about getting ahead in the world, as opposed to the one who's saving her salary for a grand wedding.

The bright ones are so much more fun in every way. They have the brain power to look at the world and decide for themselves what the rules will be instead of unthinkingly accepting the should's and shouldn't's of our culture.

HOW MANY ARE THERE?

In 1988 there will be 13 million between 18 and 24. A million will be black which makes it nearly impossible. *"12 million and counting."* Another three million are living in rural areas, impossible. *"9 million and counting."*

Deduct those in mental hospitals, jails, pregnant, or who are mentally or physically handicapped, those with an IQ below 100 and ethnics who don't date white boys. *"5 million and counting."*

Eliminate another million fatsos and uglies. *"4 million and holding." "Roger. We copy. Marriage problem."* Ten percent under 19 are married. By 24, half are married. *"Understood. Ignition. Lift off at 3 million."*

I live in a paradise full of young women, Los Angeles. The typical 7.2 here is an 8.2 in Phoenix, a 9.2 in Tulsa and she's a 10.2 anywhere in Appalachia. I've calculated there are 15,000 unmarried, average and up females 18 to 24 within ten miles of my place. Probably 5,000 are living with a guy or are about to get married. Gee whiz, shucks, gosh darn, only 10,000 to choose from. If you live in the suburbs of a large city, your choice is as wide as mine.

You say you've noticed a lot of talk about *Boyfriends*. Disillusioned? Don't be. You'll only know what really makes her tick when you find out why she has a boyfriend. He makes little difference to her. He must make no difference to you.

"O Romeo, Romeo!
wherefore art thou
Romeo?"

Juliet, for all young women

Boyfriends

After you're able to crack the 25 year old barrier you will quickly find yourself involved with a young woman who has a boyfriend. Why? Only twenty percent of the target population is without boyfriends or fiances. You won't get anywhere limiting yourself to those without.

WHY SHE HAS A BOYFRIEND

Beyond her natural need for human companionship and sex, beyond her common need to escape neurotic parents she's programmed to "need" a boyfriend. She feels it as a real need, as real, as powerful, as any natural need.

But she learns this particular "need." Her family, schools, religion, Girl Scouts, television and other institutions teach her, brainwash her into wanting what our culture blindly considers a timeless value. Coupling young and reproducing has a 50,000 year track record of success. Our customs of marriage and reproduction are based on, and rooted in, ancient tribal survival values. Those long dead rituals live today as societal pressure on the young to pair off for life and make babies.

A hundred years ago it made sense for farm families and poor families. Survival of the tribe (family) depended on the children having children quickly so there would be more workers for the fields, mines or factories.

Today it makes absolutely no sense to couple young and reproduce, yet few young women question the reasonableness of marrying one's first or second "love" and having children until it's too late. It's too late when she's 27, has two kids, he's staying out all night, there's no money and she's 40 pounds over-weight. Her intense desire to be Queen for a Day precludes rationality.

QUEEN FOR A DAY - A POWERFUL DRIVER. The girls who get married are the envy of all female friends and acquaintances. Even colleagues who realize 18 to 24 is ridiculously young to make "until death" commitments are envious. The bride is the center of attention for weeks preceding the ceremony, then she's literally, Queen for a Day.

Each and every young female in attendance yearns for the focus to be on her and they all, or nearly all, are secretly jealous and resentful. Surprisingly they feel this way even when the groom is a geek, unre-pentant womanizer, druggie or a shiftless, unemployed dolt. Every young woman wants to be Queen for a Day. A queen must have a king, any king.

MINI - ENGAGEMENTS AND MARRIAGES. For six or more years they lived in, and many still live in, a subculture dominated by peer pressure and peer values. Their entire mini-society is devoted to pairing up, rehearsing to get married and live happily ever after. As they move toward this unquestioned goal, miniature engagements and marriages give them a chance to learn, practice and perfect the control and manipulation techniques they will use in their real marriage.

Mini-engagements are marked by frat pins in the academic world. In the real world a promise ring is used, a miniature diamond set in an engagement ring mounting. How cute.

The primary reason for a mini-engagement is to make them feel like grown-ups and to cement their relationship. She uses the occasion to lord it over her girl friends and to legitimize her sexual relations. He uses it to ensure steady sex. When you see his "brand" on her one of two things will be true, she'll be impossible or relatively easy.

In my experience a third of them take him for

granted after the mini-engagement. Before hooking him she was preoccupied with getting and keeping a boyfriend but now she's free to discover the rest of the world, including older men.

Mini-marriages (living together) and most mini-engagements come complete with monogamous expectations, the requirement to only have the same friends, to visit and "enjoy" each other's parents and so on. When they break up it is a highly charged, severely painful event similar to divorce in every way, with crushed egos and dashed dreams. Even in puppy love the love is real, at least to the puppies.

WHICH ONES HAVE BOYFRIENDS?

Every 18 and 19 year old has one. In the 20 to 21 age range, the percentage without rises to ten or fifteen percent. Over 21 and under 23 year olds do without to the tune of twenty percent. There is a veritable abundance of young women without a "man" in their lives in the over 23 group, about one in three. Trouble is, there aren't many unmarried ones.

If you're dedicated to not getting involved with someone with a boyfriend, stick with those over 23. By the time they reach the quarter century mark and a few years beyond, only fifty percent are seriously involved. This cheering fact has a dark side. There are many desperate-to-get-married 25-30 year olds out there and by that age most see you as a prospect.

Bad news: the target population over 22 is halved, decimated by marriage. *Good news:* one in four of the unmarrieds, of any age, will have an affair with you, if she can keep her boyfriend. There are two kinds of girls with boyfriends, those who tell you about him and those who don't.

ANNOUNCED BOYFRIENDS. When she mentions him early on it means: (1) She's not interested. (2) She's interested, wants you to know the score. (3) She wants to flirt with you and feel serenely indignant when she wins the Rapo game. (Rapo, as in Rape-o is described fully in *Court Her.*) Seventy percent of the time it's (1). Ten percent of the time it's heavenly (2).

If she doesn't say anything about him right away but does later it means: (1) She was kinda interested and didn't want you to fade away. After getting to know you she wants to have an affair if she can keep her boyfriend. (2) She was interested but after getting to know you this is how she says no. (3) She was playing Rapo with you all along, you've made your move, this is how she says, "What kind of girl do you think I am?" (4) She likes you, doesn't want to date you but didn't feel any of her personal life was appropriate until now. It's usually (1) (2) or (3). The first two account for sixty percent.

Announced or unannounced, there are three kinds of boyfriends.

LEFTOVER BOYFRIENDS. If she's been with him since high school he's only a security blanket. He is her means of acceptance in the subculture and a sex partner but most important, a place to avoid the risks associated with growing up and becoming a self sufficient person. She takes him for granted, doesn't respect him, has only boring sex with him but she doesn't have the courage to break up and look for something better.

She announces him with, "My boyfriend and I went to Magic Mountain," or, "Jimmy and I stayed at his Grandma's cabin." The longer they've been together, the easier it is to have an affair with her.

She only wants the same thing you wanted from the women you had affairs with when married, thrills, satisfying her curiosity and uninvolved, exciting distraction.

After a couple of nights or a few weeks with you, she runs back to him. She's found out about older men and even if it was a thousand times better than with him, she is motivated by fear.

She has not been prepared by her parents or the culture to become an independent, productive adult. She was never taught the skills or attitudes needed to grow toward independence and self reliance. She has been prepared from birth for only one role. Even if you open her eyes for a brief blinding moment to other possible choices, she is overwhelmed by the heretofore unknown real world and wants no part of it. She has none of the tools needed to live there.

Even the semi-literates who watch "Donahue" and read *People* know she has a sixty percent chance of ending up back in the real world after three years of marriage. The sad part is, she will still be only a frightened teenager inside, with no job skills, no money and two kids depending on her.

Mary Ann used "my ex-boyfriend" in our first substantial conversation. At the time I only knew she wanted me to know she was available.

As it turned out she and Jimmy were just fighting, again, about his staying out all night several times a week. He decided to show her "who wears the pants in this house" and didn't come home for two weeks. She needed someone to distract her from the pain and loneliness.

After four dates in seven days, three of them full of lusty sex she had never known, I called. She said simply, "I'm back with Jimmy, can't go out anymore. Sorry. Bye."

Epilogue. She got married three months later, had a baby, then divorced within a year. She is pushing 160 pounds and lives with her child at Mom's.

Jimmy was this "dude's" real name. In his "honor" all boyfriends in this book are named Jimmy. He was, and is, typical.

Understanding The Leftover Situation. She must sneak time with you, at first risking only a few minutes. If you're relaxed, fun and appear safe, she'll stay for a couple of hours. Then she'll "go for it," spending a whole afternoon in bed with you. Evenings are too dangerous, they have established a pattern of after dinner calls, under some pretext, to check on each other.

Later, she'll make a date for the entire evening when she's figured out how to explain why she won't be home. But, she will stand you up without notice if he suspected something and "just happened" to stop by her place. When he's going to the mountains or desert with his buddies, she'll spend the night.

An affair with her can last many months if she's brighter than average and has some innate courage. A duration of anything beyond two months requires counting from the day you two end up in bed until she really quits. There is no time deduction for the in's and out's of the affair on her part.

She quits for a week, comes back for two days, quits "forever," comes back for three weeks and so on. Withdrawals and re-entries are brought on by extreme feelings which force her to re-examine her values. The conflict is sharp. Her goals are mutually exclusive: get back on track toward living happily ever after with Jimmy or continue the side trip, for awhile, with you down the road of excitement and adventure.

Like the rest of us, she wants to have her cake and eat it too. To get a clear understanding of what she goes through, see "Don's Recipe for Trouble" later in *Date Her.*

An affair of any length will be mutually rewarding if you are ethical and up front with her from the start. She learns about the real world and grows up much quicker. This wouldn't happen for years without you. In turn, she teaches you how to have fun and enjoy being carefree all over again. She gets smarter and older. You get smarter and younger. Such a deal!

She's going back to Jimmy and become Queen for a Day after a night, a week or a month. If it lasts longer than a few months she'll realize she deserves much better than Jimmy and move on.

If it's two, intense, rewarding months she starts wishing it could "lead somewhere." Ethically you must prevent this. It's hard to inject realism into the relationship once this stage is reached unless the seeds are planted early. You are the one who has to do it. (See *Ethics* and *Talk With Her.*)

STRING ALONGS - BOYFRIENDS OF CONVEN-IENCE. The young women smart enough to know marrying the Leftover is a bad idea, string him along, clinging to a corner of the security blanket while testing the waters of adult life. Also in this category are girls with any boyfriend they don't want to marry but keep for convenience.

This young woman was taught independence by her parents or became independent to survive. But, she learned self reliance in parallel with conflicting values stressing preparation for a role as wife and mother. She absorbs society's belief that her real value as a human being is ultimately measured in terms of how good a mother she becomes. So, even these, the best of the bunch, face contradictory goals before meeting you. These cause her to have conflicting goals after meeting you just like the girls with Leftovers.

This young woman outgrows males close to her age by 20 or after college. Even when she realizes how "totally out of it" boys are, she can't conceive of life without a boyfriend, so she gets an "older man" of 27, like Randy RedPorsche. After a few attempts she realizes he and his contemporaries only want to make temporary deposits in her sperm bank.

The independent young woman knows: (1) She doesn't want to marry the security blanket she's holding by a corner, although she'd love all that ceremonial attention. (2) Young men four to eight years older only use her. (3) Boys don't know what it's all about.

She wants to find out what it's really all about. At the same time part of her says she should get married and make babies, another part says to be independent and make a life for herself. Faced with this dilemma, she's ready for you.

But, from her point of view you may turn out to be a turkey or too much for her to handle. She's reluctant to burn her bridges. Besides, she'll have some functions to attend where you can't go. God forbid, she can't possibly go by herself, especially on Saturday night, Christmas or New Year's. Heavens, people would think she doesn't have a boyfriend! Branded a complete failure at 20 or 21.

The young woman with a String Along announces him in terms implying she sees other people or wants to, starting with you. Something like, "Jimmy's going to the desert this weekend, so I'm going to the Gamma's party and see what I can pick up. Hee, hee." Or, she just wears a promise ring and tells you with her body and eyes she's available.

Sometimes she announces him in terms sounding like she doesn't really have one. As a worst case example Donna said, "Jimmy? Oh, one of the guys I used to date." She wasn't really lying, he was in jail. She felt so guilty for "fooling around" she married him two weeks after he finished his sentence for stealing $60,000 from his first father-in-law!

Epilogue. He threw her out with nothing a year later after beating her severely. She got pregnant by the next guy she moved in with, trying to make him marry her. He left when she refused an abortion. At 24, she and her baby are living with her divorced sister and her three kids. She didn't get as fat as Mary Ann, only 150 pounds. But Donna started at 110, a dynamite 110, I might add. What a waste of life.

Neither Donna nor Mary Ann were future rocket scientists. But they were both plenty smart enough to not do what they did. They made long range decisions with emotions, not brains. Wanting to be Queen for a Day, is indeed, a powerful driver.

Understanding The Convenience Situation. The affair starts out awkwardly if she has not hinted or said she can't be seen with you. To save face she pretends she's not sneaking time with you. The stress is enough to ruin everything on the launching pad. My solution is to always suggest out of the way places and unusual times for initial dates.

A word of caution. Never ask directly or indirectly if she minds being seen with you or why she can't make it for a date if she calls and begs off. Don't force her to admit what she does not want to admit. It's not important.

These young women are teetering on adulthood but aren't ready to dive in. They are prone to get neurotic quickly but if you're relaxed and patient things can settle down to a moderately long relationship of say, five to eight months.

After the opening, delicate stages the affair can develop into a marvelous time for both of you. As with the girls who have to steal time and sneak around, the early stages are much the same. However, this young woman is braver, eager to get on with it, so events proceed at a more rapid pace. It's about the same as with an unattached 27 year old after the second get together, except this young woman can't be seen with you.

If you two are really enjoying each other, she too, will want it to "lead somewhere." Again, to be a stand up guy, you must plant the same seeds early on so sanity can be restored more easily if this stage is reached. (See *Ethics.)*

An affair of a couple of months with you lets her see she's ready and able to make it on her own. She breaks up with Jimmy and moves into an apartment with a girl friend. Without telling you she continues to see him, after he forgives her, but she only strings him along while dating you and others. In the end, she strings you along, too. She's braver than the ones with a death grip on the security blanket but no more honest. Neither knows how.

You are her interim-transitional "boyfriend" while she builds her confidence to live in the adult world. You're only a tour guide. Don't let this be demeaning to you or to her. She needs your support while learning. Don't forget, she's teaching you plenty, too.

Yeah, I know I didn't tell you about the third kind of boyfriend, he's explained in *The Right Attitude.* I didn't cover unannounced boyfriends either, I'm saving them for an explosive surprise later on.

Even though you now understand her better, far better than she understands herself, you won't get anywhere until you understand one other person, yourself. What you don't know can, and will, hurt you. I'm living proof as you will see, and hopefully learn from.

If you don't know why or doubt your sanity for wanting to date someone half your age you'll never be able to do it. Step one is making certain you fully accept, believe and thoroughly understand *Why Young Women* are the best females on the planet. After that comes the hard part, being honest with yourself about other motives you have.

"What a drag it is getting old."

Mick Jagger

*"A man is only as old
as the woman he feels."*

Groucho

Why Young Women

Most of my women friends and acquaintances claim they can't understand why divorced men only want to date young women. Knowing men are drawn by physical attractiveness they point out, in a thinly disguised, catty manner, "surface appearance is a shallow reason," implying they're attracted to a man by his deeper, more noble qualities. (Yeah, right! Newman and Redford are noble.)

The more intelligent ones quickly add, "female beauty is only a culturally derived aesthetic, a mere definition, artificial, learned, not reflecting reality." (So what? It's the standard everyone uses, except liberated men.)

In an attempt to convince me not to "waste time" with younger women they begin by being reasonable, "A 22 year old can't possibly appreciate a man," move up to, "A girl just can't relate fully to a man," escalate to, "A young woman does not have the experience to satisfy a man," then both barrels, "It can't lead anywhere." (Gee, how nice, they want it to lead somewhere. Do you suppose they want me to get married again, to someone their age? Hum?)

When nothing works, believing their perspective is the only one from which reality can be viewed, they retreat to, "We're rational. You're suffering from temporary insanity, acting out Middle Age Crazy." (Could be.)

Here's another perspective, possibly another reality, that of a divorced, 46 year old man. (I, too, have come a long way, baby.)

WHY YOUNG?

My young lover makes me feel my power and potency again. She causes me to experience the life and pleasure I've earned and deserve but never enjoyed.

She appreciates and respects what I've accomplished across the years. When I look in her eyes I see, reflected back, the image I want to see, one that corresponds with my self-image. To her I am a hero and a success, something my wife could never see.

I don't get compared with men my age and found lacking. When she does compare me, it's with college sophomores, then ranks me highest. Whatever I am or want to be is fine with her. No demands to grow up, come home or go to her mother's. There's no power struggle. To her, men are not the enemy.

With her I can be soft, romantic, giving and caring. She treasures these qualities in a male. I can talk with her about my second thoughts, even third thoughts on life, children and career. I don't have to be strong and rational all the time. She doesn't mind when I cry, in fact, she likes it and sees tears as merely human, not a sign of weakness or fallibility.

She wants and values her freedom as I do. Someday she wants to find Mr. Rite and get married, but for now she's not ready to settle down. She and her compatriots are free spirits still.

Two of her better qualities, ones I've never found in any woman: (1) When I don't feel like going to the office she doesn't panic and worry about money. (2) She doesn't mind if I watch the Raiders kick ass on Sunday.

WHY NOT A WOMAN 25 TO 35? Never married women over 25 insist on being serious, "Where is this leading?" If you haven't had the pleasure yet, it means, "Are we getting married?" Young women don't ask about my remarriage plans before the salad arrives.

A divorced woman in this age range is wonderful if

she doesn't look for men in a bar, if she doesn't have children and if she's not off on some liberated binge.

But, it's impossible to find a single woman under 35 who isn't in a bar smoking cigarettes one after the other, looking the males over like she's choosing her evening meal. Most want only uninvolved sex, their way of avoiding loneliness without getting hurt, again. These dick-of-the-week bar flies are big time disease carriers. No thanks. If I do manage to meet a woman in this age range, she's either living with a guy or has two children.

The ones with kids have lost their zest, lost their idealism, lost their interest in experimenting and exploring. They are tired every night. They distrust men. Some hate men and use them without blinking an eye, rationalizing it as getting even for all the suffering males have caused them.

With a young woman, "The prick didn't send my child support check" crisis doesn't exist, neither do baby sitting hassles and the other endless problems divorced mothers face. I feel for them yes, but I don't date anyone with more problems than I have.

WHY NOT A WOMAN MY AGE? In my experience most are looking for a new husband so they don't have to stay out here in this big, mean, cold, nasty, cruel world and make it. The ones not looking to get married aren't busy losing weight and getting into shape, they're grinding a feminist ax. Stuff what they say about beauty only being skin deep. Fat bellies, saggy breasts, stretch marks and wide asses are not attractive.

Women my age, and yours, expect me to be hard, strong, unemotional, rational, their knight in shining armor. I am no longer anyone's saviour or protector. I don't fix cars, washing machines or anything else unless the damsel in distress is under 25.

Harsh words, yes. They reflect what I've learned, the harsh way.

Relationships with women close to my age are, "Like, you know, totally, predictable." I know the role I'm supposed to play. She knows the role I'm supposed to play. Through subtle, and sometimes not so subtle manipulation she prevents me from being anything other than what she wants me to be, expects me to be. I end up relating to her the way I related to my former wife. There's no room for innovation or freedom, no way to stop the same old shit from happening.

Women over 35 are behavioral clones of my ex and yours, as tired, as jaded, as boring, with the same values. They're from the same era.

GREAT, NO EXPECTATIONS! If you want to be who you are now, and what you are now, you need someone from a different era, a woman who didn't grow up thinking a 40 year old man should be Ozzie Nelson. A young woman doesn't know what you're supposed to be, she has no experience with anyone your age.

To her you are an unknown, a mystery, an exciting male. You can paint yourself any way you'd like, different every day. You can be a kite flying 13 year old, an 18 year old cock hound, a daredevil of 27 and it's always okay to be a sensitive human being with feelings, frustrations, desires and dreams. You don't need shiny armor.

MY PRIMARY QUALIFICATIONS. A few years ago a woman news anchor sued a broadcaster, claiming she was fired because she wasn't pretty enough or pleasant enough. I predicted she would win, thinking not one of her male bosses had the balls to say he prefers females to be attractive and sweet tempered.

I've got 'em. "Anyone I date must be attractive and sweet tempered." I'm still able to say that because I have one more requirement, "She cannot be a castrating bitch." Since my divorce only four women over 30 had three out of three. I have yet to meet a ball buster under 24.

Thanks to "strong" women my preference has become immoral because it's anti-egalitarian. (Look at stewardesses these days. Eeccch!) As you know that news anchor eventually lost but it wasn't the result of management's truthfulness.

FAR MORE THAN BEAUTY. If you've spent the night with a divorced mother you'll recognize this "good morning" comment, "Shit, it's only Wednesday." When a young woman gets up she sees a day full of promise, something wonderful might happen.

Young women are far more of the goodness of "female," far less of the meanness. They're less angry, less hurt, less burdened, less demanding, less manipulative, more alive, more energetic, more emotional, more spontaneous, more open and yes, more attractive.

Youth is alive, excited, emotional, full of enthusiasm, energy and drive. Youth can change the world, and your world. Her positive attitude infects you. Optimism and hope cast out cynicism and futility.

When I finally made love with a young woman two long years after getting divorced, I felt whole again, reborn. By touching me, taking me inside, enjoying my thrusting, surrendering to orgasm, she anointed me. No longer a banished leper, an untouchable, unlovable, middle aged man, I was reaccepted into the human race.

Our culture values youth, period. I'm a member of our culture. I value young women, period.

THE INTERNAL ME AND MAYBE YOU

A few years ago I discovered the gut-level reason I strongly prefer young women. I used to think it was because they are so physically attractive. I used to think it was because they are so much more fun. I used to think it was because I didn't know how to date them when I was young. I used to think it was because they make me feel so male, so alive. I used to think my friends might be right about my Peter Pan syndrome, you know, never growing up. The soul-searched truth has elements of all these and little to do with any of them.

When I look in the mirror I don't see a young man looking back at me. The guy I see has thinning hair, deep wrinkles and has to lean away from the mirror to get his image in focus. Yeah, I know that middle aged man in the mirror is me but he doesn't look like the me trapped in this 46 year old body. The me inside, the real me, the emotional, spiritual me is 27 years old.

I ask you, what 27 year old wants to date a 39 year old divorcee with three kids? I want someone who doesn't look and act like she's old enough to be my mother, at least the mother of my internal self. The me inside wants the same young women the average 27 year old wants, Pets or Playmates of the Month, UCLA cheerleaders and any girl sitting by the pool in Palm Springs during Easter vacation.

As stated, I discovered all this a few years ago. I had other reasons and still have some. Let me tell you about both as you begin to *Understand Yourself.*

"Know thyself."

Socrates

Understand Yourself

If you're like me, what used to be important, isn't. A corner office with a walnut waste basket no longer has much significance. A nicely mown lawn, a clean workbench in the garage, who cares? But those young females, those beautiful, alive, young females, now they're right up there, in fact what could really be more important? Well, what?

In the year of our Lord 2016, I don't think I'll even remember how cleverly I blocked Harry's attempt to transfer [steal] part of my budget back in '79. If I do recall I doubt it will give me any pleasure even if he was a formidable corporate opponent.

Company politics and intrigue used to be fun. Damn, I used to enjoy outthinking assholes like Harry. These days I get beat often. Much more important things are on my mind, crucial decisions await. "Should I call Betsy back or let her wait a couple of hours? Maybe I ought to call Anne first, just chat, see how she's doing after our football date, check what the vibes are? Nah! I should go over there, make an appearance. I'll call Betsy later."

Last Monday morning the kiss asses were busy hovering around our alcoholic, muddle headed Division Manager, plotting their end run for Tuesday's staff meeting. Jim managed to let me know right after lunch. I could have short cut those dicks but it would have taken half the night.

My values are different now, now that I know I'm going to get old and die. I spent the rest of Monday afternoon bullshitting with Anne, the big, round, red head in Building 20. She asked me over "to watch Monday Night Football." Yeah, right.

Sure, I got blown away at the meeting. Knowing the grim reaper's waiting helped me make my choice. So I don't make Department Head, I made Anne, twice.

WITHOUT A LITTLE HELP FROM YOUR FRIENDS

Have you learned by now no one can take care of you except you? You're going to get tons of unasked for advice on how to get it back together so you can keep on keeping on. You know, how to age gracefully. Heard this yet?

> *"What's the matter with you? Act your age! Don't make a fool out of yourself. Don't embarrass us either for Christ's sake. Stop this nonsense. It can't lead anywhere. Make up with your wife. She's an understanding person. Put your life back together."*
>
> *"Wattayamean, 'Fuck off?' Maybe you should see somebody about this. You're acting crazy!"*

To be terrified of dying without ever having lived is not crazy.

A sated young lover lying in your arms, grinning a satisfied, smug smile, can prove you're not crazy quicker than any bearded, self-righteous shrink. He'll charge $50 an hour to tell you:

> *"It's okay to have these feelings. Everyone does at your age. They're just feelings. Feelings aren't wrong. Actions are wrong. Go ahead, talk about young women. It'll make you feel better. It's normal to want them."*

Puke. Double Puke. Take that $50 and buy Tracy a gold ankle chain. That's much more productive, as long as you expect nothing in return.

Maybe you are crazy. Everyone seems to think so except me and a few thousand experts on middle age. We understand. I've gone through everything you're struggling with. It didn't kill me. It hurt like hell, yes. But I'm still here and I'm going to stay here. I won't go back to a miserable, boring, empty marriage, a mind numbing career or being successful.

What good is "success" if you're miserable, bored, horny, empty and lonely? Of what use are club memberships, electronic toys and weekend cabins when you're going to die in the end? Do you want to look back and remember, "I was a big shot. My office was on the top floor with a big desk and a credenza?"

It's my turn. I paid my dues. I earned the right to exist on my terms, to be with whom I want, when I want. You must think it's your turn or you wouldn't be reading this book.

ARE YOU STILL ALIVE?

Once you know you're going to die it's natural and normal to seek reassurance you're still alive, proof you have life left to give and share. Others think we should somehow know we're alive, think we should accept middle age, old age and death gracefully. Others think, period.

Not me. I wanted to know, not think I was, and am, a desirable, alive man. I sought irrefutable, hard evidence.

When your young lover takes you into her body you'll interpret her act of giving as the ultimate evidence you are alive. She, the essence of life itself, of what it means to be alive, will prove it. Everything else will be, and is, intellectual dog shit. I interpreted it the same way.

Making passionate love with her at six on Monday morning will be reassuring with a capital R. Life will be worth living, again. She'll bring joy, pleasure, softness and innocence back into your world. You will have a reason to make money, a purpose, something to look forward to. You'll be able to go out there again, out there where mediocrity and assholes call the shots.

ANOTHER VIEWPOINT, MINE

Seen the movie Middle Age Crazy? It's true except for the money grubbing "happy" ending. He resigns himself to spending the rest of his life in suburbia after reconciling with his wife. Screw that.

The way I look at it you can go back to being married any time. You can go back to dating divorced women with kids anytime. At 40, time's running out for young women.

You'll never have another chance like this. You can still get your body into good condition so she's attracted to you on a physical level. At 55 I doubt it, unless you're John Derek or Dorian Gray. Although you're on the down hill side of athletic prowess you can still make love like an 18 year old, when she's 20.

It's your life, what's left of it. The next ten years can be the best decade of your life if, and only if, *Your Motives* are ethical and practical.

*"There are few,
if any, accidents."*

Freud

Your Motives

What do you want from a young woman, anyway? Do you want to have stimulating conversations about competing anthropological theories on the origins of religion? Do you want her to be a sparkling, cultured hostess to help clinch your next big deal by charming your clients? Perhaps you'd like a female who'd do your laundry, clean your house, feed the dog, do the shopping, service your sexual needs without complaint and never ask for money.

You're reading the wrong book, Jack!

SPELL IT OUT

Define what you want. Don't be shy. Tell it like it is. Sex, companionship, understanding, friendship? You can want anything. A sex partner, a lover, a friend.

Maybe you'd like a: fiance, steady girl friend, nearly steady girl friend, part-time girl friend, serious date, frequent date, semi-frequent date, life partner, casual lover. How 'bout just a torrid affair? A female you can control? A date for the weekend with no questions asked on Monday morning?

Okay, so you're reluctant. I'll go first, so you get the idea. I want a female unencumbered by children who does not want to get encumbered. I want her to be unjaded and optimistic. I want a someone who is aroused easily, excited by sex because she hasn't done this a hundred times before.

I want somebody I can be silly with, play with, laugh with, someone carefree, untroubled. I want a young woman I can talk to when I'm troubled and get things off my chest, cry if I have to. She needs to listen empathetically but she doesn't have to understand.

I don't want someone to clean and cook for me. I don't want a live-in lover. I don't want a girl friend, steady or unsteady. I don't want to be a provider. I don't want to be considered a potential husband.

Got the idea? Well, what do you want? Be honest. You don't have to be realistic but you must know why you're doing this. If you don't, you'll soon wonder why it's so dark, not knowing your head is up your ass.

WHAT A YOUNG WOMAN CANNOT BE

She can't be a woman. She can't be your equal. She can't be an adult capable of long term planning. She can't know what you already know. She can't understand what you already understand. She can't give up her dreams for you. She is a package deal.

She can't be your wife or live-in lover unless you're into long term frustration and pain. She can't be an understanding friend, even if she can be your friend, as she has no real grasp of adult problems, trials and frustrations.

UNREALISTIC MOTIVES

Like many things you do, your desire to date young women is often driven by something you may not be aware of. The big three motives men hide from themselves:

Proving you are still a man.
Hurting your ex-wife.
Trying to recover a lost youth.

The first is everyone's favorite, foolish, often necessary but unless you're carefully honest, it makes you a user of the worst kind. The second is popular, a natural want but demonstrates you are a complete asshole as well as a user of the worst kind. The third, impossible, sometimes required before you can move on. It's the most dangerous to you and your young lover. Before getting into the big three, here are some other classics.

If you just want some "young stuff" wear a wedding

band, act like you're married, behave like you only want to get laid. It's easy if you're slim and trim, looking good and over your divorce. (That's all explained a couple of chapters from now.)

If you're not slim et al, and you still just want to get laid, hire expensive, young prostitutes. It's honest. The energy, time and money saved will be tremendous, not to mention the frustration, ridicule and pain you'll spare yourself.

If you're looking for a meaningful, long term, love relationship, only date women over 30. If you want to be taken care of by a substitute mother, stick with women over 35.

HURTING YOUR EX-WIFE. If you're driven by wanting to anger and hurt your ex, believe me, I understand, sympathize and empathize. Here is a much more ethical and effective way of doing it. Get a beautiful prostitute who doesn't look like a whore. Arrange to be seen with her where the news will travel fast, twice a week for a month.

Moneywise, you'll be way ahead even if she's $100 per hour. We're talking, what? $300 a week for a month? Shit, you'll spend that much just on clothes getting ready for young women. And don't forget fringe bennies. The rental girl will get you off ten times better than any 22 year old you'll ever meet.

You won't have to wait until you're over the divorce so you can behave like a confident, together, mature male, mandatory to attract young women. That seems to take a year or two. You won't have to wait until you get rid of that pot belly and learn how to dress, which takes another six months. But if you wait that long you won't give a shit what your ex thinks anyway.

Seriously now, if getting even with your ex is a primary motive, you won't be worth a good goddamn meeting and dating young women anyway. Just lose weight, get in shape, learn how to look good, then after a year of 35 year old divorcees you'll be properly motivated.

PROVING YOU'RE STILL A MAN. You are a man. In reality there's nothing to prove, to anyone. It doesn't feel that way inside you say. Yep, I remember.

To feel like a man completely, you must have direct, tangible evidence females are attracted to you and desire you. Not just any female, either. The more attractive and desirable the female, the more you feel like a man. Okay, I'll buy that.

We know, in our culture, how old the most attractive, desirable females are. We know how females directly and tangibly give hard evidence you are attractive and desirable. And, we know you doubt your manliness, shaken by divorce and looming middle age.

Now we know one of your motives for wanting to date young women, don't we? You want to prove you're still are a virile male with plenty of miles left on your cock.

Okay, it's true. You want to feel like a man again. So what? Big fuckin' deal. Every one of the million and a half guys each year who ends up where you are wants the same damn thing. Now the only question is, will you be honorable as you gather the evidence needed to feel like a man?

If you're not honest and realistic with your young lover, and with yourself, about the long run impossibilities of your affair, you will dishonorably hurt and scar her. You need only one thing to be honorable, honesty. To be honest you need courage. Either you have both or you will never, ever feel like a man.

TRYING TO RECOVER A LOST YOUTH. Above I said "impossible." That's not strong enough. I tried "harebrained" "impractical" and "unachievable." Then decided there isn't a word strong enough to stop you from trying. So, I'll tell you my story. That won't stop you either. It may make it easier for you to honestly search your heart and come to a level of awareness and self acceptance years sooner, with far less heartache for you and your young lover.

With the help of a strong, honest, smart 24 year old who didn't want to get "too involved," I became aware I really wasn't just having fun and enjoying life with young women.

I was shocked. She was right. I was trying to make her my girl friend. Damn. How could I have not known that? I worried about it a lot. I questioned myself. I talked about it. I thought about it, then I had a second thought: "Who gives a shit how sane, reasonable or productive my needs, wants and desires are. I have them and by god I'm going to fulfill them."

A year later I fell in love with a 19 year old. I didn't just fall in love, I dived in love, with abandon. I had a hidden motive.

HIDDEN MOTIVES

"There's many a change in the winter wind,
And a change in the cloud's design.
There's many a change in a young [girl's] heart,
But never a change in mine."

I Never Will Marry - American Traditional

I've been at this long enough to make every mistake possible, the biggest one twice. From ultra-sad experience I can tell you a young woman is not able to give you the storybook marriage you may still long for, as I did, and do.

You remember, back in the '50's, the marriage our society indoctrinated us with, lead us to believe in, to seek, to die for. We saw it in movies, read about it in fairy tales. Prince Charming marries Cinderella and they live happily ever after.

In my heart of hearts that's the marriage I still want no matter how cynical I appear to be, no matter how unrealistic and unattainable that marriage is. I bought that dream. It is locked in my every muscle, burned in every fiber of my heart. I want it. I deserve it. I earned it. I feel cheated my life did not turn out that way.

You may have a hidden primary motive for dating young women. I discovered mine when, for the second time, I was devastated emotionally and spiritually crushed by a young woman. My will to live was at the low point of my entire 45 years. I had no purpose, no goal, no hope. I would never have my dream marriage, ever. Life was futile. Why bother?

After partially recovering, a two month process, I asked myself, "What am I doing wrong? How could I pick a second young woman to fall madly, totally, in love with, who would break my heart?" I knew it couldn't be the gods were testing me again. It had to be me, something I was doing. I chose both of them from the entire Los Angeles population.

What did they have in common? Personality-wise, absolutely nothing. The first was a quiet introvert, the second a funny extrovert. Physically, absolutely nothing. A beautiful, tall, thin blond, and a short, round brunette with a different face. They were both very bright. They were both ex-Catholics. So what?

I opened my reluctant eyes. They were both 19 when I fell uncommittedly in love with them. I married the first when I was 36. I wanted to marry the second when I was 46!

YOU CAN'T GO HOME AGAIN. My hidden motive was to find a young wife, so I could go back and re-live my adult life. It hadn't turned out like it was supposed to. Goddamnit! Life was going to give me what I longed for and believed in, a happily-ever-after dream marriage.

This time I was ready. There would be no way of messing up. I knew too much, everything I'd learned from two marriages plus all the knowledge gathered during 44 years on the planet.

Our marriage wasn't going to be the idiotic impossible kind I was raised believing in. Shit, I knew that wasn't reality. No couple can do that, not even Ozzie and Harriet. This marriage was going to be custom made, designed to fit both our needs. We were going to live happily for as long as possible, then call it quits. Realistic. Practical. We'd have each other as friends, lovers and partners. What could have been better? A chance to go back and do it over, the right way.

You're the only guy who knows what your motives really are. I didn't take time to look at mine, too busy looking for a young wife. Take the time. Have the courage to look genuinely and deeply inside yourself. It is not shameful to long for a chance to live life over again. It is foolish to try. Why is it?

Only Change Is Constant. Think back. Wasn't it light years from 16 to 21? Remember who you were at 21. Were you anything like that at 30? What's important to a 19 year old is insignificant to a 25 year old.

You are nearly the person you'll be for the rest of your life. At 21 or 22, she's beginning to become the person she'll be. At her age she changes ten times faster than you. After a year with you her goals, world view, sexual needs and lust for life will be so different from the girl you fell in love with your head will spin. In the decade ahead she will become a completely different human being, emotionally, spiritually and psychologically. Each day she will gain more self knowledge and self confidence. Her horizons will broaden. Life's possibilities will become numerous and real to her. Her goals will change. Her values will change. She will judge you by those new values.

Sure, being with her across time will change you, it will change you radically. But not enough or fast enough to keep up with her. Even if you like the new her, she won't like you. She wants more. More what she doesn't know. She only knows you can't give it to her.

I married Sharon when she was 23. I was 36. We divorced when she was 29. We never had a chance. The years from 23 to 29 are five times more change-filled than those from 36 to 42. We had two years of happiness, a year of boring neutrality and ended with three years of misery.

I met Carla on her 19th birthday. I fell self abandonedly, madly, totally in love with her two months later. I let love come like a giant tsunami wave, crash over me and sweep me away, reborn. Just like in the movies.

The joy of life she brought. Her face lighting up

like a Christmas tree when I'd please her. What pleasure, just talking and being with her. What happiness. What lack of emptiness. This was the one I was looking for, the young wife who could give me one more chance at living my life over.

What did I do? Pressured her subtly and not so subtly to return my love. What did she do? Picked fights so she could break up with me or hurt me so much I'd break up with her. We had a romantic but stormy, on again-off again 18 month affair until finally, she quit, fed up with it all.

Without her I had no plan, no dream. I was lost. I promised to stop talking about living together, to stop thinking about the future and live our affair one day at a time. Miracle of miracles it worked for three great months. Then her boyfriend dumped her, "To find out who I am."

Two weeks later she said she'd like to work toward living together. Jesus! Did I leap in, heart and soul! During the next two months it became painfully, ever so painfully apparent, she was not interested, willing or capable of sustaining a relationship with me or anyone else, for that matter.

She hurt me so deeply and so often by lying during that time, she destroyed all love I had for her. I felt like such a fool. I wanted to die.

Later, I could see she had been totally confused about life, love, sex and commitment. She'd made that offer only to ensure I'd be there for her like a devoted puppy until she decided what she wanted from life, boys, young men and men. I was a convenient anchor, nothing more.

If Carla and I had married her changes would have made Sharon's look like minor ripples. Carla was so much stronger and braver. She would have stretched herself farther and faster, growing more, changing more, becoming more each year until she moved on.

Since Carla, I am able to simply enjoy what my young lovers have to offer. As always, I'm honest, ethical and fair. If I start falling in love I diplomatically reduce the intensity level, so as not to make her feel rejected. If she insists on knowing why I am backing off, I tactfully tell her what I've learned about myself from Carla and my unrealistic motives for loving a young woman and hope she continues at a reduced pace.

And yet I still find, back there in the corner of my heart, a longing for a young wife so I can try again. I stay aware of my motive and of the impossibilities. When I start feeling like I may be slipping over the abyss, I look in the mirror and shout, "Say, fool! She's twenty goddamned years old. Let's not go on that trip, again. Just enjoy, while it lasts."

You'll hear more about Carla later on. There were plenty of good times, too. But, right now, it's time to *Get Ready For Her.*

*"The first attraction
was purely physical."*

Rod Stewart

*"There's no such thing
as luck, only preparation
meeting opportunity."*

Coach Lombardi

Get Ready For Her

Soon you'll have to talk with her about things she's interested in. First you must look like somebody she'd like to talk to. *Translation:* Someone she'd like on top of her.

Let's not bullshit ourselves, okay? She's already what you want. You have to become what she wants. Lard disgusts her!

SLIM AND TRIM

You're not even ready to talk with her until you're within ten pounds of your weight at the end of boot camp. You don't need muscles, you need to be slim and trim. Either get there or buy a video of *"Teen Nymphos Unchained"* and whack off to it for the rest of your life.

There's only one way to lose weight: eat less and exercise more. Only running works. It's effective, measurable. There's no way to rationalize. You can run anywhere, anytime with nothing but a pair of $30 shoes. Bicycling, skiing, tennis, swimming, racket ball and so on, are pseudo exercise with built-in excuses.

Fuck dieting. Stop eating so goddamn much. Get your fat ass out there and put those miles on. Everything else is self deception.

A six percent weight loss is "well on your way." If after two months of running and eating less, you aren't well on your way to slim and trim, you're not serious. Resign yourself to divorcees over 35. They don't mind fat, it mixes well with theirs.

Be intelligent about it. You took ten years to get so flabby and out of shape, don't try to get back to your fighting weight in a couple of months. Buy some books. Develop a plan, a schedule and a daily routine with measurable, yet attainable goals. Everything in your life has to be adjusted to your fitness program. Nothing interferes, not dating, not work, not travel, not holidays. Only resolve and perseverance works.

When you can run thirty minutes a day, at a ten minute per mile pace join a coed aerobic exercise class. Keep running on the days it doesn't meet but get in that class, you'll meet some new friends of both sexes, under 30.

YOUNG FRIENDS. Making friends with as many young people as possible is the second most important part of getting ready for her. You know what's the most important don't you, Beer Belly. While you're getting trimmed down find, meet, talk with and become friends with anyone under 30.

Smile and say hello to young folks at work, coming and going around your complex and especially at any gathering, social or otherwise. This makes it much easier to start a conversation with him or her when you meet again.

Young females are reluctant to talk with any male who approaches them, let alone a 40 year old potential masher. But when you merely know someone she does, you have a built in "reference," you're not an undesirable of any kind, reducing her tension and fear quickly. The more fear you can keep out of the initial encounter, the easier it is to attract her.

Take junior college or college classes both sexes under 30 will be in. During the semester young people will relax and open up to you if you act like an equal. At semester's end you will be invited to a celebration where you'll have a chance to become good friends with those on your wavelength.

I took Film and Television Production, Radio Production, Film as Literature and Photography. I made a lifelong female and male friend. They formed the core of my after-divorce circle.

Join a health club. Visit several close to home or work. Choose one that's not a pickup bar without the bar. Get to know all young males. Make friends with the ones you like.

Invite young men to watch football or any other sport for that matter, get to know each other better. Drink beer, talk and tell jokes and other "manly" pastimes. They'll get to see you're a normal person. You'll get used to young people.

After you are friends with a guy under 30 the entire process becomes so much easier. When he introduces you it's a stamp of approval from the anti-dirty old man league. The young women in his circles accept you quickly if you're friendly and aren't on the make. Eventually lightning will strike.

REAL WORLD SUCCESS STORY. Last week I went to the supermarket to grab some beer for the Monday night game. Jenny, from my film class, was working as a box girl. I stopped and chatted with her on the way in. On my way out the cute cashier said, "Hi, Don," and gave me a big smile. I raced through my memory banks searching for a name or where, or when, or how she knew me. At Mark's party? The college workshop last month? Blank, nothing! Shit!

I glanced at her name tag. "Cathy? Sorry. I don't remember you." She laughed and told me she'd asked Jenny who I was. We talked a bit and I left. I went back to her checkout stand the next day and the next and the next.

On Sunday we went to brunch and talked, got to know each other. She was about to be engaged to her boyfriend, away at school. Without saying so she wanted to have a fling before she settled down. I obliged her, happily.

You never know when the gods will provide the opportunity. I was prepared. I'd paid my dues with Jenny.

READY TO TALK. If you can't talk with women you can't talk with young women. Read, *How to Talk to Anybody about Anything*, by Barbara Walters. Learn how to converse, with women first.

If you can talk to women without getting tongue tied or inappropriately suggestive, you only need to learn about things that interest young women. Get informed. You don't have to become an expert but don't be ignorant like her father. You'll highlight the age difference.

What's an 18 to 24 year old interested in? Clothes, males, music, cars, movies, television, skiing, travel, partying, drinking and drugs. Okay, now that you know what her interests are, what do you already know she might find interesting? Even better, what does she know you can learn from her?

Set some of your car radio pushbuttons to her music stations. Make yourself listen. Pick out the music you like. Buy the "artist's" albums and tapes.

She doesn't expect you to be into her music but if you demonstrate knowledge of the current music scene you will impress her quickly. Burn your Elvis and Sinatra albums or put them in the garage where she'll never see them.

You might not be able to discuss Prince, Madonna or Depeche Mode. At least you won't have a blank look on your face when she's talking about them. You may not like the rockers she does but you'll know who they are so you won't be like Daddy or her teachers. You will be different, one of the most important keys to being able to date young women.

CH, CH, CH, CHANGES. When you're almost down to boot camp weight change everything. Change restaurants, coffee shops, bars, social clubs, spa, everything. The young women who already know you are not going to be interested just because you finally got it together.

Interview with several new companies as you're getting the flab off. Pick the one with the largest number of young females on the payroll. If that's not possible, change divisions of your present company.

Don't go until you're slim and trim.

If you stay at the same company, forget it. It's too late. All the young ones have seen how you look at them. They've seen you fat and dressed like a dork. They won't care if you change now.

The typical, southern California, divorced 40 year old buys a red Porsche and moves to an apartment complex in Marina Del Rey, the singles' capital of the world. After two months of trying he wonders why he can't get anywhere. The people who live in these places are pro's, solid plastic. They read *Playboy's* "Hottest Pickup Bars In the Country," then rush to the closest.

You can't find a better way of meeting a young woman than at a friend's house. The quickest and best way is to move to an apartment or condo complex where most tenants are 25 to 40. The best would be one of those apartment buildings next to the college, if it's not ninety percent students. The noise would be overwhelming and you'd look out of place, thus suspicious.

Find a place where the people are not swinging singles. Talk to everyone at work. Ask around. Read the ads. Then get up off you ass and go out looking. Don't bother moving in until you're slim and trim. You don't want to make any poor first impressions.

YO' RIDE, BRO'. For all her young life boys have talked and talked about cars. She accepts the importance of a male having a cool car.

Your wheels are important, not crucial like your slim, trim figure and dressing well, but don't drive something that reeks of middle age. If you have a four-door Olds, sell it and buy something comparably priced that's sporty or has some class. Don't spend big bucks on a car expecting her to go for you because of what you drive unless you want to attract gold diggers.

Your car can be too young: VW Rabbit or bug, 914 Porsche, Vega, Pinto, MG Midget, little pickup truck or any cheap, tiny car. It can be too old, literally if it's faded and worn or, figuratively, like a nine-passenger station wagon. It can be too ostentatious like a Cadillac or big Mercedes. She hates big cars, even convertibles or T-tops such as Eldorados or Lincolns unless it's trendy as '59 Caddies are now (1985).

BMW's, Volvos, Saab Turbos and Mercedes 190's are the current Yuppie loves. They'll do fine if you can make yourself join the pack. Touring cars are double barreled, classy and sporty: Porsche 944's, 300 ZX's, Vettes, Jag XJS's, Maseratis, dream on.

Sporty two door cars like the Supra, Accord, Impulse and T-Bird all are good choices. Acceptable sporty/classy four door sedans are made by: Jag, Volvo, BMW, Mazda, Honda and the sporty American iron (mid-size only).

You must have a "totally bitchin'" stereo. She loves her music loud and sounding good. Anything over $300 will do. Do not overextend your finances. Save your money to spend on far more important and productive things in the future, like flying with her to Las Vegas. Young competitors can't catch you after that, no matter what they're driving.

YOUR PLACE. Don't have a faggot decorate it for you. 'Spress yo'sef. You don't have to have expensive furniture. You must have a great stereo and her music. A good television and stereo VCR are helpful. Dressing well is far more important if bucks are tight.

Your bedroom must not look like a pleasure palace. Water beds arouse suspicions. Masculine and comfortable, period. No mirrors!

Keep your place neat and clean. There is no better first impression you can make on a young woman than to have a well kept home. She's used to the filth young men live in. And, she's used to being expected to clean their dumps when she visits them. Don't even ask her to help straighten up until the third month, then be extremely polite.

Most young women love champagne. They think it's romantic. Pragmatic is what I think. The carbonation gets the alcohol into her blood stream faster. I keep two bottles in my refrigerator at all times. They love junk food. Once she's there don't interrupt the flow to go out. Stock up, then keep your fat hands off it.

SMOKE. Get rid of your cigars, period. Pipes are just as bad except for the rare young woman who fantasizes making it with a professor-type. Only stink up the garage until she mentions liking pipes.

Cigarettes are another story. She will not hold it against you if you don't smoke. Many dislike cigarettes so much they will dismiss you instantly if you smoke, about thirty percent I'd guess. The rest either smoke or don't care. Don't, until you see her lighting up or until you can find out where she is on this intensely emotional issue.

Most don't care if you get high smoking marijuana. Eighty percent will join you. I estimate only five percent will reject you for altering your perception. I've never met one. About half of the ones who smoke dope will tease you about being a wimp if you don't but none will hold it against you.

DRUGS. Alcohol is her favorite drug. She likes everything from beer to Long Island Iced Teas. Younger or less experienced ones prefer foo-foo drinks. I've never even met one who didn't drink.

After you start moving in younger circles you will be able to buy anything, including heroin, within a few hours of asking around among people who trust you. If you were into the Sammy Suburbia-Harriet Housewife scene during the 60's and 70's you are a potential drug experimenter. I've abandoned all except Miller Lite, cheap champagne and Kona Gold.

Young women, especially independent ones interested in an affair with and older man, take drugs for the thrill of it and to test themselves. Many love cocaine, some to the point of ruining their lives. None will write you off for not snorting but some consider you a heroin addict if you whiff a couple of lines.

This is an issue requiring a sensitive approach. Younger females aren't different from older ones in this area. However you deal with women and cocaine is fine. Young people are not the Hoover vacuums portrayed in the media. I strongly recommend never touching the stuff.

Speed and downers in all forms are used by fifteen percent in my experience. They won't hold it against you for not ingesting these chemicals or any others, if you don't preach.

Some young women take drugs to escape from a too painful reality. Between 1979 and 1982 I saw a beautiful young woman end up on heroin, another end up in jail with her boyfriend dead of an overdose. Someone with a drug problem may be attracted to you. You can play savior or bail out early. In my experience you can't save anyone.

BUSINESS CARD. Design a classy, tasteful, expensive, interesting business card. It is a present to her, your first. It separates you from the boys and makes her feel grownup and important. Make it something to talk about. Cute, different, unusual.

READY TO SHAKE. You must have a firm, masculine hand shake. If you don't, develop one. Have the balls to get advice from your female friends. You needn't say what you practicing for. Feedback is necessary to change. (Much more on shaking hands with her is coming in *Court Her.*)

You can do everything in this chapter while losing that gut, then you'll need a whole new wardrobe to start *Looking Good.*

"The clothes make the man."

Unknown wise person

"Brown Shoes Don't Make It"

Frank Zappa

Looking Good

The young woman out there waiting for you is infatuated with clothes. She talks about them, reads about them, loves shopping for them and appreciates any man who wears them well.

You won't get anywhere looking like her Daddy. Gather up all Daddy-look-a-like clothes. Don't put them in a bag for the Salvation Army. Burn them. Burn them right now, like evidence convicting you of father rape and mother murder.

Next, buy and read thoroughly, *Dressing Right* by C. Hix, published by St. Martin's and *What Women Really Want in Men*, published by Playboy Press. Pay attention to how male models 35 to 60 are dressed in magazines like *Playboy, Esquire* and *Gentleman's Quarterly*. Don't be trendy, follow fashion.

After you've read the books and understand the principles involved get up off your wallet and go shopping. If you have a young female friend, or even one who's a burned out hulk of 28, take her along. Tell her you want truthful opinions and advice. If you don't have an under-30 friend, enlist an acquaintance but friends are best. They aren't afraid to tell it like it is.

DRESSING WELL

You must look good and dress well all the time if you're serious. That doesn't mean jacket and tie. It means wearing tasteful, fashionable clothing, appropriate to the situation.

I suggest you dress as sharply as possible based on what the situation permits. In some settings T-shirts are fine but a polo shirt would not be over dressed but sharper, especially the color you look best in. I get the most compliments in dark green and black. You know what yours are. It gives you an edge. W. C. Fields and I only want "a fair advantage."

Being overdressed gives the impression you are stuffy, the kiss of death to under-25 possibilities. Daddy is stuffy. Teachers are stuffy. You're a casual, relaxed man who just happens to be 20 years older than she is. Dress the part.

Never, never leave the house without being well dressed even if you are only going to the supermarket. The one time you don't take those ten extra minutes to look good will be the day Laurie Longleggs is working as cashier, alone, bored and only you to talk with.

Clothes will not make you look younger. She views a man of 40 dressed like a 22 year old the same way you look at a fiftyish woman in a mini-skirt. Besides turning her off, it will cause you to be secretly ridiculed everywhere, including your company. Don't make a fool out of yourself on purpose, you'll do enough of that by accident on this quest.

ABSOLUTE NO NO'S. Before I get into it, re-read Zappa's quote above. Brown shoes are worn only with beige or brown attire. Got it? Brown belts, brown socks, brown jackets, brown any damn thing, only goes with brown. There are a few exceptions, read the books.

The recommended books are excellent but they concentrate on the "do's." Here are my biggest "don't's."

To avoid looking like her Daddy, a pathetic Sugar Daddy or just a putz, never wear bright colors or anything blatantly polyester. Avoid the rest of these the same way you avoid women who are fat, angry ball busters:

Two-tone shoes including golf shoes, aloha shirts, any hat, ball caps under-30 year olds wear, long boxer underwear, white jockey underwear, any undershirt, Bermuda shorts, Speedo trunks, patent leather shoes, elevator shoes, high heels, plaid or patterned pants or jackets, loud ties, white or pastel suits, most cowboy boots, tank tops, muscle shirts, bedroom slippers, sandals with socks, Beatle boots, Wallabys, Top Siders, Hush Puppies, pajamas, jump suits, suspenders, pants pocket handkerchiefs, shawl sweaters, button front sleeveless sweaters, matching warmup suits and any 60's or 70's attire such as bell bottoms or tie-dyed T-shirts.

The books cover accessories well but as a rule, "When in doubt, do without." Mandatory do-without's:

Gold chains, pinky rings, gaudy, gold ostentatious watches and rings, gold bracelets. . . *Time out!*

If you're wearing more than $200 worth of jewelry and accessories, including the wrist watch, you're trying to impress her with your money. You want her to want you, not what you can buy her. Let the fat, phony, pricks driving Mercedes 500 SEC's behave like that. They're the ones who must buy her. *Time in!*

Any necklace, glasses on a string around your neck, lapel buttons, large belt buckles, half-lens glasses, paging beepers, sweat bands or head bands, clip on tie, any tie clasp or tack, calculator watches, shirt pocket-protecting pen holders and any 60's or 70's ornamentation like turquoise, silver or beads.

There are hundreds of other no no's. Pay attention to the models in the magazines mentioned. Study "the look," copy it at first, later, develop your own.

PLASTIC SURGERY

Face and eye lifts are for men obsessed with wrinkles. If you fit in this category don't go for the economy model. Go to the same doctors the stars do, and then only after considering carefully why Charles Bronson doesn't bother.

But wait, this is not something to joke about. Plastic surgery, even to get rid of the bags under one's eyes is a serious matter. Doctors screw up just like auto mechanics. This is a decision requiring extensive investigation. My advice is: don't take a chance until you're 55 and look 75. I have three women friends who have had plastic surgery. After two operations one now has tits she can live with. The others had bad experiences even after going to the best in Beverly Hills.

The first "only" had her crow's feet "fixed" for $3000. She now looks scared all the time. After crying a lot she's suing. The other had her nose "fixed." After winning a three year legal battle she had to go through it two more times. I think she looked better before. If it ain't broke, don't "fix" it.

HAIR

Don't comb your hair in an elaborate way to "disguise" your bald spot or receding hair line. That has the same impact on her as wearing white patent leather shoes, lime green leisure suit, open shirt, five gold chains, a gold nugget watch and a diamond pinky ring, Instant Dry Pussy.

If you want her to have the same physiological response, wear a toupee.

Hair transplants, hair weaving and other "new" methods to make your hair thicker only make your wallet thinner. Forget it. You need your money for much more important matters, like taking her to Palm Springs.

Any young woman you talk with does not expect you to have a full head of hair. She wants you to be real, to be a man. Boys have hair, men do sometimes. She wants a man, not a boy. Hair, or the lack of it, does not make the man, his clothes do.

For those of us getting thin on top short hair is mandatory. It gives the appearance of more. Short means, short all over. Not short with forty long hairs combed back in the middle or other futile attempt to pretend your hair is not down the shower drain.

For those with plenty of hair, shorter hair is still

the best. It makes you look younger. The length depends on the shape of your face and neck. The best hair style is one that looks natural and casual, bordering on wind blown. Study the models in the magazines.

The well dressed man never looks like he needs a hair cut or like he just got one. Don't be shaggy or have "white walls."

Unless you work for IBM, don't taper the hair around your ears and in the back like a conservative business man. No 50's hair styles either, especially anything resembling our heros, James Dean, Elvis, Fabian. The 60's and 70's are out, too. Mick Jagger, Bob Dylan, Frank Zappa, et al are has been's. Get with it.

Anything that looks styled dates you, then you don't date her. Hair helmets were popular in the early 70's and are worn by men still living in the early 70's. Their hair is straightened by blow drying, styled over the ears, edges turned under, then frozen in place with hair spray. Jimmy Carter's 1976 campaign photo is The Hair Helmet. Jack Kemp was wearing one a couple of years ago, now I don't know. I've lost interest in such trivial shit like who's president. I'm focused on bigger things, younger things.

Colored hair on you, contrary to the ads, looks as phony to her as bleached or blue hair does to you. The slightest bit of artificiality prevents verbal intercourse leading to the other kind of intercourse. She thinks, "If he dyes his hair, he needs a penile implant."

Gray and graying hair is a magnet, if you've got a decent body to go with it. If you don't, she only sees a fat, old man. Your slim, trim body comes first with her. If it happens to be attached to gray hair, all the better.

HAIR ON YOUR FACE. Facial hair makes you look older. It also makes you look like a leftover hippy. Don't date yourself. You'll only date your fist. Sideburns are useless, except in Tulsa or Appalachia. If you live either place move first, then take time to shave.

Trying to compensate for a bald head with a beard only looks like you're trying to compensate for a bald head with a beard. Mustaches or beards make you more attractive if you have certain facial features. Do without unless you have an upper lip a mile wide or no chin.

If your features require facial hair it must be neat, short and well trimmed at all times. Don't sit at the table wondering why she's smirking. There's a piece of fettucini hung up in your 'stash. Constant monitoring is required when eating or drinking. The rest of the time, combing and constant grooming is a must.

Blade shaving seems to take off a couple of years. I do it in the morning or before she comes over in the evening. The rest of the time I use the Norelco in the car and shave on the way to the supermarket, coffee shop, restaurant or sporting goods store. I never know who may be working there.

HAIR ON THE REST OF YOUR HEAD. The hormonal changes you begin around 35 and continue through 55 make you want to fuck like an 18 year old. That's good. The same changes cause hair in your ears and nose to grow like Topsy. That's bad.

Don't let her find a bush in your ear when she slips her tongue in there. (You know what I was going say about her bush and your tongue, don't you?) Hairs sticking out of your nose are as attractive as a booger. Trim all these hairs every damned week. Develop a routine. Don't you dare forget. "Yucky" is her descriptive word for these hairs. Bushy eyebrows must be trimmed. No discussion.

BODY HAIR. Thick back hair or chest hair protruding from your shirt makes you look like a gorilla. Keep it trimmed. It appeals only to Middle Easterners. I have no interest in them. Racist? Nope. I know who I like, it's never anyone who can't speak the king's English.

MOUTH AND TEETH

Tobacco stained, broken, poorly capped or missing teeth put you in the infamous lime green leisure suit and cause the same vaginal response. So will ill fitting or obvious dentures. Don't make her dry on purpose, you'll do enough of that accidentally.

A great smile is worth the bucks. Ask around for the best cosmetic dentist. With denture problems find the one who fits them for the rich people in your area. If you're still in Appalachia after what I said about sideburns, you're out of luck, but don't worry, bad teeth fit in there, fine.

Keep your teeth clean, breath smelling sweet at all times. Don't be looking good then ruin a chance meeting with Nancy Nicetits because you have halitosis or food stuck between your chompers.

GLASSES

If you can wear contacts get rid of your glasses. Consider some of the tinted ones. Don't try to be a Paul Newman look-alike. Anything even slightly phony puts her on guard.

If you can see fairly well without glasses, wear them as little as possible. Squinting to see her across the room is not attractive, however.

Trendy glasses are always wrong, as is anything trendy. Glasses that look old fashioned are always wrong, as is everything old fashioned. Old fashioned to her is five years ago. Lenses that change darkness with the lighting conditions are simply dorky.

Wearing bifocals or trifocals is like rolling over to her in a wheel chair with a shawl on and saying, "That dimple on your left knee is absolutely sensational." If you need glasses to read, get some that don't look like reading glasses.

Don't have any glasses, including sunglasses, on a string around your neck. Only old men or Disco Dicks do. Don't push your glasses up on your forehead, only old men do. Don't push your sunglasses up on top of your head, only Westwood Ass Holes and Disco Dicks do.

Go to a place specializing in fitting glasses when you're happy with your prescription. Ask the salesperson for advice based on the shape of your face and try on several varieties of the recommended frame. Then, try on every other shape, style and color in the place. Look in the mirror. Ask the sales-person's opinion. If you can't decide buy several different styles and see which get the best reactions during the next few weeks. Get reading glasses in the same styles. Pick out some frames for prescription sunglasses when you're there. You may look better in "shades" of a different shape. Experiment.

Never wear mirrored lenses. Females distrust you, thinking you're staring while hiding. If you like to girl watch, just do it. It turns many on if you aren't blatantly crotch gazing.

Keep your glasses clean. It turns her off to look into your eyes only to notice how grubby your glasses are.

EVERYTHING ELSE

A sun tan is a solid "fair advantage." In winter go to a tanning salon but avoid the plastic people who are always there. The rest of the year get your ass outside as often as possible or, if you live in the Sun Belt, eat lunch outside when possible. That's what I do.

Neatly trimmed, clean finger nails are mandatory. Her boyfriend's are always dirty from working on his cool car. Young women notice everything. You're so different, they're always checking you out, comparing you to a young man.

Louise once told me toes looked "like an old man's." My routine of trimming them every Sunday before a 10 K had been disrupted for a couple of months while I let a sprain heal.

Buy and use expensive cologne all the time. I have a bottle in my car, another in my office desk.

THIS LOOK IS ONLY TEMPORARY

Most of my advice helps you prevent her from having the physiological reaction mentioned. The look and principles described in the recommended books aid in attracting the largest number of females under 25 but it has a wonderful side effect, it attracts far more over 25, making the upcoming advice in *Women First* much easier to follow.

Eventually, you must express your individual tastes

and the person you are with your clothes and overall appearance. Your goal is to find and date a young woman who likes you as you are, not the you dressed by the book.

Young women prefer an older lover who wears a uniform of sorts: GQ model, tennis bum, cowboy, macho cop, business man, professor, movie producer, trucker, aging rock star, or whomever you are or want to become. I'm a kicked-back Hawaii-to-mainland transplant when not in the office. At work, I'm a semi-traditional business man with a soft edge.

Gradually begin modifying the prescribed look to one expressing your personality. Stay within my bounds and those in the two suggested books for at least six months, a year at most. Then, 'spress yo'sef.

While you're slimming down, dress well and always look good. At the same time you can you can begin to develop *The Right Attitude*.

The Right Attitude

Without the right attitude you won't get anywhere even if you are slim and trim, looking good, living in the right complex, driving a beige Jag, listening to her music, working in a new company, partying with young friends and dating 32 year olds.

Young women are attracted to a man who won't kiss ass. They are strongly drawn by indifference, feigned or real. She will date you, an older man, only if you're friendly, aloof, relaxed, powerful and confident. Your unspoken attitude is: "I am the catch here, not you. I'm not going to chase you. Sure I'm friendly, I'm friendly with all the girls. Yeah, I'm somewhat interested. It might be possible if you, young lady, play your cards right. Well, gotta go, there's a nice young woman waiting for me. Catch you later. By the way, you're not bad."

Later, it's still unspoken: "Going out with me is natural. I'm attracted to you, you're attracted to me. You have a choice, a man or lots of boys. Well, gotta go, there's a nice young woman waiting for me. She likes what I do with her. You will too, when you grow up."

And even later, still unspoken, it's: "If not tonight, no biggie, we will. I'm in no hurry. Let's watch tv for awhile."

Finally, spoken, it's: "No. I have plans tonight. Look, I've said this before. I don't like anyone coming over without calling first. Please don't do it again, okay. What? Sure, I'll call you."

MR. CLUTCH'S ATTITUDE

You're old enough to remember Jerry West. If you ever caught one of his interviews you saw The Right Attitude I'm describing. He was friendly, relaxed and slow. He was not impressed with himself or his ability. To him it was merely a fact, simply the truth, he was the best ever. To unseeing eyes he seemed humble, he wasn't. He was confident, genuinely confident.

But notice in his quote above, "tried." He knew, and accepted, that once in a while he didn't have The Right Attitude. Neither do I and neither will you. Even if talking with a young women is "just a game" too, it feels like life or death the first, oh, two or three hundred times.

TWO KINDS OF ADVICE

I don't offer useless advice like "Don't be afraid." Selling books with idiotic counsel like that is fraud, at a minimum. There's no hidden button you can push and become unafraid. Of course you're scared, it's all new, the rules are unknown. You might get laughed at or even slapped.

When first meeting and talking with a young woman I'm always nervous. Opportunity without danger is only a pushover. I am not completely confident now and never expect to be. I'm preaching reality. You'll never "... *pick up girls. By the truckloads,*" neither will Weber or any cretin who tries one of his "lines."

My advice is simply to tell you what the right attitude is, then explain how you begin developing it. You'll never get there, since development is an ongoing never-ending process. You only get better, never perfect.

STEP ONE - FEELING LIKE AN EQUAL. Developing the right attitude begins with the belief and the inner feeling you're the equal of young people. If you think your age makes you better, you won't get anywhere. If you feel inferior to youth, you will be.

When you doubt your equality she will pick up those vibrations and turn you down. *Achtung!* You vil follow orders as given in "Young Friends." Being around youth day and night lets you see, feel and believe, they're not much different, you've just had more birthday parties.

My First Step. Long ago and far away in another life I decided to go after some "young stuff." I was forty pounds overweight, couldn't run around the block, had a corner office with ulcer, dressed in polyester, wore sideburns and mustache, drove a Sedan De Ville, lived "in the heights," listened to dentist-office musak and was unhappily married.

I felt old, acted old, thought old and was old, in spirit. In fact, I was 32 going on 52. I felt inferior to youth. They had, both males and females, something magical, something I'd lost half my life ago. I wanted it back. Deeply fearing I'd be rejected and laughed at, I had to force myself.

I began at work, going out of my way to say hello and be friendly with anyone under 35. Eventually I made friends with a 20 year old receptionist. Within weeks she introduced me to many other young people.

Six months later I was running 10 k's every Sunday with some "dudes" from work. A month after that I was drinking beer with them at their parties where I met and talked with females 16 to 25.

I didn't get anywhere, afraid to try. But just by talking with these young women I grew accustomed to youth and was able to relax in their presence. After a few months I realized they weren't superior to me but my Jesus, were they ever superior to older females.

A few months later I was able to approach and have secret, pure sex affairs with several young women at the office. As you know by now they were with me because I was married, not in spite of it. But at least I got started. Somehow, some way, you have to get started, then end up feeling like an equal, too.

STEP TWO - SLOW AND EASY. I'm never rock solid confident even after all these years in the arena. You're never going to be completely confident either, so work on being slow. Confident people are not in a hurry, not pushy, not nervous or excited. Moving slowly and talking slowly at least gives the appearance of confidence. First impressions are lasting impressions. Take your time.

Waiting to talk to her is not what I mean by taking your time. If you go into her work and she's busy, conduct your business with someone else and leave. You're confident. If not today, tomorrow. If not her, then Stacy or Gina.

STEP THREE - CATCH 22. It's just like trying to get your first real job, not the one as a box boy. "Have you ever been an Assistant Manager? You haven't. Sorry, we're only hiring experienced personnel."

Here's the circular trap when trying to date young women. Success comes only from being relaxed and confident. Relaxation comes only from confidence. Confidence comes only from success.

Therefore, you must start out pretending to be confident, so you can be successful, then you can relax because you're confident. You create the required, self sustaining loop of success-confidence-relaxation by: *Achtung!* You vil do as ordered in *Women First*.

The campaign to gain self assurance is done slowly. It is a two pronged attack. You are relearning dating skills and building confidence in yourself as a man. There's only one way to learn, by doing.

A preview of *Women First*. After you've been dating Maggie, 34, for a few months you'll have the confidence needed to start courting Darlene, 28, night manager at the restaurant you've been going to for three months. Five months later, when you're dating Darlene, start working on Jean, the 23 year old at the bank and Kathy, 22, over in Payroll.

You can only climb back down one rung at a time. You begin with women, gradually working your way down to 20 year olds. If you're a real masochist you keep going down until you're happy you can attract 18 year olds.

A good fight manager builds his young boxer's experience slowly, never overmatching him, not giving him pushovers. He doesn't want his boy to take a whuppin' and lose his confidence. He doesn't want him to have false confidence, either.

Build your confidence, don't crush it. Think about it. Plan it. Schedule it. Don't be in a hurry, neither Rome nor Roberta were made in a day.

If you have an unrealistic or hidden motive driving your desire for young women you will never develop the right attitude.

STEP FOUR - YOU GOTTA KNOW WHEN TO FOLD 'EM. Much of the right attitude is your willingness to walk away from her. You must do it, not just imply it. In fact, this has to be your attitude the entire time you're in the relationship with her otherwise she'll climb into the driver's seat. (Much, much more later in *Who's In Charge Here?*)

I had been working on Marilyn for a couple of months. She was strongly interested and showed it by touching me often as we talked and bumping me with her delightful, tiny tits, "accidentally." I suggested a drink after work. She brought a teddy bear, Stephanie.

The next week we arranged another date. She didn't show. A few days later she apologized with a weak excuse. She still touched me a lot with several body parts. I only smiled and waited.

After a week she asked me to Sunday brunch. I told her I was busy, which was the truth. The Raiders were on at ten, the Cowboys at one. "Maybe some other time. Gotta go."

Don't be anxious or too interested. I probably would have gone to brunch if I had not been dating Tina, then it would not have turned out as it did.

Two weeks later Marilyn asked to come over to my place "just for one drink." Two days later she spent the night. Folding your hand works sometimes. Nothing else ever works.

STEP FIVE - UNDERSTANDING THE COMPET-ITORS. Having the right attitude means you know who and what you're up against. You don't overestimate, you don't underestimate. You understand the realities, then and accept or decline the challenge.

Boyfriends As Competitors. Remember Leftovers and String Alongs. With them it's boy against man. Knowledge and experience versus ineptitude and ignorance. Fear not. Your lack of hair and slow reloading time mean nothing. Both Leftovers and String Alongs are either studs or duds or shits.

Jimmy Studly. After a year she's only a source of steady pussy. He's only interested in shooting his load and getting back to his four wheelin' buddies. Studly's concerned with what they think as he "proves" to himself he's a "man." She's just a girl, what would she know about "men?" Wouldn't he be surprised?

Jimmy Dudly. The nice young man. He's wants to marry her and have babies. He's loving and caring but she dominates him, controls him and doesn't respect him. He's her safety net. She sees him only as a "fer sure" date when she needs one. She'll lie and use him all the time. But when he gets tired of it, meets someone new and quits, she'll go after him with everything she's got, with no time for you. Don't make an ass out of yourself, move on.

Jimmy Shitly. There's one more kind of boyfriend, the guy who treats her like dog shit. He keeps her under his thumb, begging for more while he does exactly as he pleases with other girls and with his buddies.

This guy's easy to cut in on but it's impossible to keep dancing with her. After a month you'll be so glad to hear her proudly announce, "I've absolutely, finally broken it off with Shitly."

In a couple of days Shitly will be a little drunk and secretly want a blow job. He'll call her at two in the morning, crying, promising to change. She'll rush to him and drain him completely, happy to reward him for finally becoming the man she wanted all along.

Two days later, at a party where others will notice, he'll bang Debbie, her best friend. Crushed, disbelieving, she'll come back to you, until he calls, again.

When Shitly's in the picture, change channels.

Mr. Rite. The young woman without a boyfriend will drop you like a rock for Mr. Rite. You have no chance against him. He has two qualities you don't, marriable and marriable. Once she meets him you're history. Don't behave like a dick. You knew the score.

Young Husbands. Avoid married young females like you avoid the girl who says, "It's only a cold sore." When he finds out he will be humiliated and enraged far beyond her cheating with just another boy. The young husband knows he, himself, is just another boy. He can't compete with you, thus must eliminate you (kill your ass, in plain English) or her, or both of you!

STEP SIX - ACCEPTING YOUR FAIR ADVANTAGE. Be realistic, you have the edge over all boys and young men. You have far more experience with life, sex, money, travel and females. You have acquired some "class" with your age. You reek with natural power and don't have to be a braggart.

Money alone puts you in a different league. Expensive cologne smells ten times better than his Brut. You can go to fine restaurants any night, not just after the Spring Formal. The two of you can spend the night at a luxury hotel, right on the water, just for the fun of it. Money makes it possible to travel with her to faraway places with strange sounding names like Hawaii, Tahoe or Las Vegas.

Let's take cologne as an example. Young women, no, any female over 17 has a keen sense of smell, enabling her to recognize and appreciate the better fragrances. Once she "picks up your scent" she's instantly aware you're different and something special. How's that for an edge right out of the chute? Don't leave home without it! Not even to run down to the market.

But you know all this. I want you to feel confident because I guaran-god-damn-tee you'll need it in abundance.

The best and biggest edge, you're a gentleman. You light her cigarette, open her car door, hold her chair, order for her, wait until she lifts her fork and all other manners discarded by most men, including me for awhile, at the demand of "strong" women in the 70's.

You register at a hotel with her at your side without becoming anxious like Jimmy does. That's a first class hotel, of course. You don't lecture her on why she should have taken her car to the gas station instead of to the dealer, as he does to prove he's so smart. You don't grab her tit in public and laugh about it. You know how to listen and empathize when she needs to get something off her chest. You're different. More later.

You are perceived by her as powerful, not physically, but powerful in dealing with life, with her, with anything. Females of all ages are attracted by power. As one Hank Kissenger called it, "the ultimate aphrodisiac."

Don't brag. Don't put down the competition. Confident men don't have to.

Your clothes make it easy for her to quickly notice you and then realize she's looking at an exceptional male. They immediately recognize, appreciate, admire and are attracted to a well dressed man. Make certain you're always well dressed. Ensure you have this particular "fair advantage" in Phase One and Phase Two.

ON NOT BEING TOO NICE

"Treat me mean, treat me cruel,
but love me."

Elvis

This is not the seventh step. Not being too nice is a mandatory, all inclusive dictate you must follow to have the right attitude.

She wants you to treat her nicely, fairly and with

respect. What you consider nice, fair and respectful is not what she expects. Why? Because your young lover is an individual human being with her own story to tell, her own personal goals, values and morals, just like you. She has a unique history of bad and good times with males, beginning with Daddy.

I love being nice. It is my nature to be nice to anyone I like and even more so, to young women I enjoy. By "nice" I mean considerate, polite, open, vulnerable, giving, attentive, appreciative, warm, accepting, gentle, demonstrative and expressive with my affection, and such.

During the early aftermath of my divorce I found women over 30 to be unappreciative, even offended by my tendency in this area. I hopefully expected younger females to appreciate my niceness. I was shocked and disappointed. Nearly all find this behavior unacceptable in any male. There have been a couple of wonderful exceptions but even those young women resisted being treated well at first.

WHY IT'S NOT IMPORTANT.   Meeting someone nice disorients her. I don't know if she thinks it's too good to be true. I do know many young women saw me as a wimp or pussy-whippable and lost respect, as well as interest, quickly. How do I know? Because I got tired of striking out and asked in simple English, "What did I do wrong?" Good old feedback.

There are two possibilities. One, she's been treated poorly for so long by Daddy and her boyfriends, it seems normal, manly. Two, she's had her ass kissed so long she's tired of it. Jimmy adores her. Daddy spoils her. She wants you to "act like a man." Who knows? Who cares? Nice does not work.

ONLY COMMODES ACCOMODATE. Being accommodating is absolutely the kiss of death. You know, adjusting your schedule to hers or even something as unimportant as yielding to her choice for Chinese over Mexican. "Commode" sounds like "accommodate." Use this memory association technique to prevent your affair from ending up in the shitter.

Just Don't Do It. In the beginning it was so delightful to finally be around them, talking and flirting but not yet dating. I was so happy I'd be nice as well as accommodating. Even though I'd learned not to, the hard way, with women, I returned to my natural ways. WRONG!

Eventually, she may be able to accept your nice treatment of her, phone calls just to talk, flowers, back rubs, presents and so forth. But early on she will simply drop you.

Part of her motive for talking with you is the challenge. She wants to see if she can get you. Don't disappoint her by being no contest. It goes along with the concept of aloofness I preach. It stimulates them. I enjoy stimulating them in every possible manner.

I resist my strong desire to be nice until we've dated at least four or five times. After that, I'm only one tenth as nice as I'd like to be. Once in awhile I still lose control if she's my cup of tea. Of course she backs off. Then I have to go out of my way to be indifferent, even mean, followed by days of being "too busy" attempting to get things back to the way they were, enjoyable.

Often this maneuver works. Sometimes it doesn't because your niceness damaged the relationship forever. *Translation*: She lost respect for you. I learned from my second marriage it is not productive for either myself or the horse, to beat a dead one. Chalk it up, move on.

REAL WORLD LESSON - ROUND ONE

Mary was 25, beautiful, six feet tall, with an ass that made me cry, bright and extroverted. A solid 9.65 on my scale. We worked at the same company. I had my eyes on her near the end of my marriage but during those final months I had no energy or capability to go after her. I did talk casually with her as often as possible, indicating my interest obliquely.

After my divorce, when I was semi-back together, I went for her. On the second date she confessed she had been interested in me for a long time but knew I was married, so controlled herself, saying she had been burned by a married lover once before. She paused, looked at me in an unusual way, then said, "And besides, I was living with my boyfriend," pause, beat, beat, look of hopeful approval, "and I still do." "Now?" I blurted, finding it incongruous single people "fooled around" like married ones. Jesus, was I naive!

She quickly explained she wanted to go out with me but wanted to be honest about her situation. Okay, no problem. I was accommodating to the max. We went out on her schedule, where she wanted, when she wanted, cost was no object, ad nauseam.

On the fifth and final date of round one she said she didn't want to see me any more, offering she didn't enjoy being with me because I made her so nervous. "Okay," what else could an accommodating person mutter, right?

ROUND TWO. Eight months later I had changed companies and finally gotten the message not to be nice after receiving it several more times from other young women. She let a friend of mine know she was living alone and wanted to see me. We went out.

I related to this 9.65 like she was a 6.0, moderately interested, somewhat aloof but pleasant. After two lunch dates she was standing in my kitchen with her blouse unbuttoned, her lipstick smeared over both our faces, working on her third Margarita and rubbing her crotch against my thigh while I caressed those magnificent buns.

I took her hand and started for the bedroom. She held back, "I have to tell you something." Being aloof and indifferent I said, "You're a virgin and you want me to be gentle?" No, that wasn't it. She had herpes but right now it wasn't active. I said, "Okay," and started for the bedroom. She resisted, sat down.

She told me, awkwardly, it's wasn't just herpes holding her back. She also had venereal warts, a vaginal infection and she might be pregnant, "I thought you'd want to know, first." I didn't scream, "No Shit, Sherlock!" like I wanted to but stayed in the living room and tactfully inquired who had caused all her problems.

The live-in boyfriend was responsible for the herpes

and warts. Her married lover for the suspected pregnancy. (Yes, the married lover she had been burned by before.) I didn't inquire about the infection, got us another drink and wondered how long she'd hang around. She got the hint and split twenty minutes later.

You can see why Mary didn't have the slightest idea what to do with someone treating her nice. Mary is not typical. She represents, in the extreme, just how rotten some of them are treated. Either she was used to it and considered it normal or she didn't have enough self respect to insist on being dealt with like a human being. I never bothered finding out.

Okay. You know what the right attitude is. You know everything else needed to court her except why it's *Women First.*

*"Eighth, and lastly,
they are so grateful."*

Ben Franklin

Women First

I've assumed your courtship skills are corroded and useless after ten or twenty years of marriage. (If you easily date 27 year olds skip this section.)

A relaxed, confident manner is mandatory to date young women. Catch 22, again. Relaxation comes from confidence which comes from repeated success. Nothing succeeds like success is not an empty phrase.

Re-learn social skills and build your confidence by courting only those females you have a good chance of being successful with. If you insist on beginning with young women or not spending enough time mastering the fundamentals, you'll get a good whuppin'. Be a good fight manager-promoter, don't over-match yourself, younger is harder.

Sure, at your age, it's humiliating, frustrating, expensive, corny, lonely, painful, et al. But relearn you must, if you're ever going date that 22 year old, red headed receptionist at your dentist's office. You know, Ginny, the friendly one with the big white teeth, big green eyes, big soft tits and big round ass.

WOMEN DEFINED

Women are over 30, divorced or living apart from a former live-in lover and have supported themselves for five years. Women are realistic about money, time and sex, as well as what's possible with you. They know who they are. They're more comfortable with and accepting of themselves as human beings. They worry far less about inconsequential matters and keep a long range perspective on life. They permit themselves to be different, resisting trends and fads.

A woman looks at the world and sees something similar to what you and I see. She is not cynical but she's not brimming with optimism and hope as a young woman is. She has picked out her niche or is working on it.

START WITH WOMEN

You can't go directly from high school to Dodger Stadium. You have to pay your dues in the minors. But don't wait until you're setting the bush league on fire batting .473. When you're able to partially function in the next lower age bracket, move.

You can't play, let alone score, in the majors until you can hit big league fast balls. But you can't even get wood on a high hard one until you've stood in the batter's box and seen, again and again, the heaters, as well as the junk, not to mention the curves thrown by younger women.

You'll get suckered by those curves and kiss the dirt, especially after you've been beaned a couple of times. But hey, Reggie's been hit, Carew was brushed back, Rose got fooled by change ups and everyone's waved at Fernando's screwgee. Not many bat over .250. My average is only .190 even after I've learned to patiently wait for my kind of pitch. *Translation:* until she shows interest. Much more in *Court Her* and *Meet Her*.

Beginning with women reduces the pressure. When there's less at stake you're relaxed, you function better, so you're successful. Catch 22 defeated.

It's easy to meet women. You're surrounded by them at work and within your existing circles, giving you a far wider selection. If you don't do well with the first, there are second, third and forth choices waiting in the wings.

WOMEN YOU'LL DATE. You will meet four types of women, all divorced. I doubt you'll meet a woman who never married, I didn't.

The Ex-housewife. After years of being only a housewife and mother she has a hard time accepting single status when it comes. She doesn't know much about the real world and how to survive. She's frightened of the future and doubts her ability to handle the problems and responsibilities facing her.

She's bitter about life and resents men. In spite of this, she wants another husband as soon as possible, so she's willing to date recently divorced men.

This woman, even if she's been on her own for a couple of years, is quite young socially because she was stuck at home for ten or fifteen years. So, she'll teach you the crucial importance of taking your time and being patient, required courtship skills for young women.

If recently divorced, she's as uncomfortable about dating as you, so she's an understanding person. She will help you get past the fear of approaching and talking with a female. This is a first step, something every journey requires.

Since I told you of her quest for a new husband you won't blow up when she wants to know your plans for remarriage before the salad arrives, right? You'll just tactfully use my answers to inevitable questions, later in the book and ask her to, "Pass the salt, please."

The Swingin' Single. She avoided the housewife trap. She's far less frightened of going it alone and doesn't usually turn out to be a secret man hater. She's not looking for another husband right away, if ever. Her agenda is similar to yours. If she's been divorced less than two years she's making up for lost time and lost youth by dating and mating with acceptable males at every opportunity.

This woman and her "sisters" can help you the most as you ease down the age ladder because she insists on ritualized preliminaries requiring the male be confident, casual and indifferent. She doesn't mind if you pretend but you must have that attitude. The good news is the prancing and dancing phase can be as short as twenty minutes, after you get the hang of it.

These women are nearly all shallow and defensive. They weren't that way when divorced. They changed for self protection. You can inadvertently pick up a disastrous idea about younger women from these swinging singles. You may think all single females behave and believe as these people do. Wrong. Young women are nothing like them except you need to be confident.

Although much of what you learn meeting and talking with them is directly applicable to young women, this phase and these women will be hard on you. Occasionally your ego will get smashed and your feelings brutalized. Some of them are unbelievably cold and dishonest. This is only a learning stopover on the way down. Don't let the overall phoniness be discouraging, as there are some, a few, genuinely nice ones. Don't spend more than four months dating swingin' singles. Too much time here will make you as hard, cruel and phony as they are, then you'll have no chance with real females, young, or any others.

Old Girls. She's an immature female in an aging body, a divorcee who hasn't grasped the essence of the real world. She's trying to live the happy single life she fantasized about when married.

This "girl's" hallmark is irresponsibility in general, financially in particular. She's moving back in with her parent(s) at age 32. She lost her job for being absent too often, staying up all night snorting coke.

Her ex wonders where the money went. She blew half the settlement on a new wardrobe, new furniture, new stereo, new television, new refrigerator, new everything. She blew half of what was left going to Hawaii for a month, "I deserved a vacation." After returning, she got rid of the rest as the down for a red 300 Turbo ZX and the first and last, plus security deposit to move into the Singles Sanctuary Luxury Apartments in Marina Del Rey.

The rent was $875 plus utilities. The car payments were $630. Her salary is a whoppin' $2300 a month.

These females are useless in your re-education process. They have all the bad qualities of young women and none of the good ones. Excuse yourself to get some more ice for your drink when she begins telling you what bad luck she's been having.

The Independent Woman.   Women divorced for a long time, ex-housewives or not, are self sufficient. Their agenda includes enjoying life, period. They are much more selective about men since they are content to be alone, not attempting to make up for anything. They are interested only in stable, long term relationships and judge you accordingly.

She seldom dates anyone divorced less than a couple of years, having learned the hard way, these men are troubled and trouble. She's the easiest to talk with but spots bullshit at fifty yards, having heard it all before. She doesn't require affected behavior. She insists on sincerity.

You can have the most fun and learn much about yourself dating these women, from 45 to 30. That's after you're able to go out with one more than three times. When you can, if she's close to 30, you're ready for the Almost Women.

STARTING AT THE TOP

Each fifth birthday puts a woman into a different courtship group: 30 to 34, 35 to 39, 40 to 45, and over 45. I didn't make up these brackets, that's the way she sees herself and the way society regards her.

Mistakes teach. Learn from every one you make. Each of us learns at a different pace and each of us has a different tolerance for failure. Adjust your descent down the age ladder to stay slightly above the failure rate you can endure.

If you've been divorced for a year, aren't an emotional basket case and look under 50, begin with the 35 to 39 group. (Those who don't meet these requirements have to begin higher on the ladder.) After a relatively short time, a wild ass guess is six months, you can slide down to the 30 to 34 age range if you've mastered the basics: find-meet-talk-date.

While dating 30-34 year olds you will learn how women spiritually far younger than you think, behave and what they value. An added benefit is meeting and making friends with even younger people. Another wild ass guess, it'll take you a year at this level before you assault the under 30 barrier.

You can begin with 30 to 34 year olds if you look under 40 unless you are a wreck emotionally. Spend a year. You'll be doing four things at once: re-learning meeting and dating; developing the right attitude, outlook and behavior toward females in general; learning from your mistakes; and making young friends.

Remember, no more than a few months with Swingin' Singles in any age bracket. You're learning how to relate to real females.

THE BIG BREAKTHROUGH - ALMOST WOMEN. You can meet and talk with these, next to the best, females only if you've made friends with younger people. You'll be able to date them if, and only if, you're easily dating women 30 to 35.

Although they have much more experience with how the world really works, compared with their younger counterparts, most retain many of the nicer qualities of youth. Their tastes in clothes, music and males is radically different from women's.

They relate to men more like coeds than women a few years older. It will be easier, later, to date 22 and 23 year olds than the first 27 year old. Don't whine, just pay your dues.

The ones who have never been married get possessive quickly. You're only a bit too old to marry. Who knows, you may just fall in love and never make it down to the next rung.

The more recent her divorce, the crazier it gets. During the first year she regresses to 20 or 21, even if approaching 30. It's her way of making up for a lost youth. You should know exactly how she feels.

The 29 Year Old - A Special Case. Divorced or never married, she faces an emotional upheaval similar to the mid-life crisis we males confront. This woman is offended by someone your age attempting to date her. Your interest is hard evidence she's not young any longer. Don't take it personally when she rudely rejects you. She doesn't have any more against you as a human being than you have against women over 40. You should know exactly how she feels.

WARNING!

Want a .357 hole in your chest? Date any separated, not divorced, woman. You can get two holes in you chest if you go out with anyone involved in a custody battle. Go to her place. Her ex's ego and dreams have been crushed. He's waiting to see who comes out of her apartment between midnight and six in the morning. The younger he is the more dangerous he is. If he's a cop, fireman or any other "macho man" you're dead. Do not get involved with these women.

LOSE A BATTLE, WIN THE WAR

If you can't get anywhere when you move into a lower bracket your attitude, outlook and manner are lacking. It could be you went down the ladder too fast. Or, you could simply be an asshole. Just wanted to make sure you're paying attention. Move back up a rung. Re-establish your confidence. No war was ever won without a single retreat.

But, this war is different. Since you're a man, not a boy, and she's only a young woman, you must have *Ethics* and not play by the rule Disco Dick and everyone else is following, "All's fair . . . ."

Ethics

Call off the battle of the sexes. Young women don't know there's a war going on.

You're entering a world where the females are harmless and defenseless. They have thin walls, minor wounds, small combat scars, little animosity toward males and few manipulative techniques you haven't see before. *Noblesse oblige.* In this case, knowledge *oblige.*

Any knowledge can be used for good or evil. You can drive an ambulance or a getaway car. How you use what you know determines your worth as a man. That's man, as in hu-man being. Conduct yourself ethically. Deserve her trust. Enjoy her, don't use her.

Your relationship with her is one of unequals. The inequality dictates you take responsibility, ensuring everything's conducted in an ethical manner. Honesty and fair play on your part is mandatory, no matter what she does.

I'm committed to honesty, tactful honesty of course, in any human relationship. I learned that the hard way, too. Dishonesty ruins everything and makes any relationship, especially a caring one, a disgusting, hypocritical sham, a waste of time. Relations with the Internal Revenue Service are the exception.

When you get to *Talk With Her* you will find ethical answers to inevitable questions. I tell you there, as I tell you here, it is not necessary to lie. It is not honorable to lie and it's not effective to lie, about anything. Don't lie.

In *Court Her* you will find out why it is not even

necessary or productive to mislead her. But, the most important reason is: you have to look yourself in the eye, in the mirror, every morning. You want to see a man, as in hu-man being looking back. Besides, honesty works, nothing else does.

You don't have to slap her face with, "Hey baby, this can't last. I'm way too old to marry you." But you are absolutely honor bound to plant seeds of thought early on so they have time to sprout into the concepts needed to re-orient her if she starts wishing it could "lead somewhere."

Seed 1. No, I don't have a girl friend. Don't like 'em, gets too complicated, just like to have fun and enjoy life.

Seed 2. I propose a toast. To a grand time, for as long as it lasts.

Seed 3. Yeah, I've had a couple [affairs]. What happened? Oh, you know, times change, people change. I'm gonna make another drink. Want one?

Seed 4. What happened with Bobbi and me? It was great for oh, 'bout seven months. She started acting like I was her boyfriend. We'd talked and stuff but oh well, times change, people change. Whose turn is it? Did I move that forty two?

Seed 5. My second wife? Too young I guess, changed a lot faster than I did, ended up wanting to have a baby. Silence. . . What? Oh sure, we'd talked, had an agreement, no kids but people change you know, forget what they said.

Seed 6. I have plans Wednesday. How 'bout Saturday?

Seed 7. I don't like it when anyone comes over without calling. Please don't do it again. (The first time quietly, the second time loudly with four letter words.)

Seed 8. Where was I all weekend? Silence. . . What's the matter? Well uh, it's getting, uh well, you're acting like I'm your boyfriend. (The second time delete the "uh's," add "I don't think this is working.")

Since I've tried the impossible twice I don't let

myself get too far down the road toward emotional entanglement. You'll learn that, the hard way, too.

AN ETHICAL AFFAIR WITH HER

A grand symbiosis takes place. She teaches you how to enjoy the now, you teach her how the world really works.

She's not your final destination, only a joyous way station on your road to oblivion. You are not her final destination either. You're only a pleasant way station on her road to marriage, children and living happily ever after.

Share your knowledge of business, people, parents, young men, college and practical solutions to her life problems. There is a wonderful, mutually rewarding time to be had by both of you as you help her discover The Joy of How Life Really Works. Part of what you bring to this party is your ability to show her what she may not find out for eight more years without you.

In return, she shares her optimism, enthusiasm, intensity, silliness, playfulness, responsiveness and acceptance of you as a human being. There is a wonderful, mutually rewarding time to be had by both of you as she helps you discover The Joy of Living, again. Part of what she brings to this party is her ability to show you what you will never find out without her.

MIGHT MAKES RIGHT. The strongest males get the best females. It's always been that way, it is that way and it will always be that way.

Stronger/older male-younger/best female was going on 50 million years before Neanderthal. It goes on openly in all societies of our primate relatives, somewhat openly in our middle class and blatantly in our "highest" society. It will be going on eons after you are recycled as worm shit. Live now but play fair.

VIRGINS ARE ONLY FOR BOYFRIENDS. Some wit once said, "I don't see why malnutrition isn't a virtue when chastity is."

A virgin doesn't get the joke. She has values and beliefs radically different from yours and thus, is incompatible with you, at a minimum. She believes with all her heart she has a gift of immeasurable worth and expects something equally valuable in return, like marriage.

Virginity indicates a severe religious upbringing or a lack of sensuality or plenty of neurosis, usually all three. A young woman in this state is someone you must only feel sorry for. Her spirit and mind are distorted, her values, beliefs and goals are in direct contradiction with nature. She is abnormal.

She is five years away from being capable of an affair with a man. That's right, five years away from being capable of learning, understanding and enjoying an older lover without being scarred and damaged. You are not to "help" her. She must find her way back to reality without you. She needs a boyfriend, a real boyfriend, not a man to help her work this out.

If you'd even consider deflowering a young woman, may your nuts fall off, tonight.

BIRTH CONTROL. The year you read this book twelve percent of unmarried females under 21 will get knocked up. They all know about contraceptives but few of the younger ones use any, feeling like they're committing premeditated fornication. The ones slightly older hope the boy will protect them. Strangely enough, even intelligent ones play Vatican Roulette, preferring the rhythm method to blatant responsibility, like the pill.

You are responsible for not impregnating her. You are responsible for determining if she's on the pill or if she's lying. You are responsible for diplomatically bringing up the subject at an appropriate time, not three seconds before penetration. You are responsible for being prepared, vasectomy, spermicide suppositories, foam or condoms.

You are responsible for everything. She's a young woman, you are a man. Remember that as you *Court Her.*

*"There are two phases
of a relationship.
Phase One is everything
before penetration.
Phase Two is everything after."*

Unknown Wise Person

Court Her

Courtship is practiced by all species in which the male is a supplicant, that is, the female does not instinctively and actively seek copulation. Each species has a ritual that must be followed carefully for the male to be permitted to mount and penetrate. The rituals all involve displays of dominance and aggressiveness on the part of the male, reluctance and submissiveness on the part of the female.

Adult gorillas take five hours to complete an intricate dance of gestures and branch waving. That's four hours longer than it takes to conduct the Westwood single's rituals of: Lying About What You Do For MGM, Mentioning Your BMW With Alpine Stereo, Flashing Your Gold American Express Card, Talking About How Boring Aspen Was, Ad Nauseam. All that, just to get herpes.

AGGRESSIVE MALES

Females of all species except one, refuse to mate with non-aggressive males. The exception is homo sapiens. Luckily the aberration is mostly limited to neurotic, ball busters past 30. You will get nowhere with young women if you are not aggressive. They have not lived long enough to become crazy enough to seek a passive male. They have only limited courting experience and no knowledge of how or when to be the aggressor or even how to be an equal. They've always been the submissive one except on rare occasions when attracted to the shy boy at school. And then they were only aggressive enough to start a conversation or two until he got the idea, then they sat back and let the "man" be in charge, "the way it's supposed to be."

TOO OLD TO MARRY HER, NOW WHAT?

The young woman you've chosen has what thousands of competing males from 15 to 80 want. What will convince her to give it to you when she know's there are no wedding bells in your future? The answer has two parts. Part One: She must think having an affair with you is her idea. Part Two: She must have at least the fantasy possibility of a romance with you before she will have an affair.

You must be aggressive to get things underway. Then you have to slow down and court her. Just be your silly old self and have fun with her until she discovers it would be wonderful to have an affair with you. Part One solved.

Young women do not see intercourse as the purpose of courtship. Their ultimate destination is the altar. To solve Part Two, you just don't burst her bubble. During the early stages of courtship you must not say, "I'm never getting married again," you dare not show obvious interest in other females and you cannot be smooth and experienced.

In her head and heart she knows the realistic chances of a life long romance with you are slim. Don't lie, cheat, steal or manipulate. When she's ready to have an affair, she will create "the fantasy possibility" so she can rationalize and proceed. Keep this in mind as you read from here to the end of the book. See how everything is designed to let, not make, these two things happen.

COURTSHIP BY CONVERSATIONS

We humans conduct courtship by talking. The complex but mandatory, ritualistic displays of dominance and submission, aggression, reluctance and reassurance all take place during conversation. Although the words you and she choose are important, even critical, most communicating is done with facial expression, tone of voice, posture and the manner of touching.

Buy, don't borrow, as many books on body language

as you can find. Read them thoroughly. Study women, young women and girls engaged in conversation with a male of any age. Don't listen to the words, watch both people. Begin to notice the exchange of signals. The only book that's useless is *Body Language* by Fast. (It's by a writer who interviewed experts and then presented his disguised opinions as fact. Ever heard of that before?)

Used book stores have them. It's worth $100 to get the non-verbal language of courtship down pat. Watch females talking everywhere, anywhere until you're able to instinctively tell when she's interested in the male she's talking with.

A MINI-SCENARIO. You approach her, an act of aggression. She smiles, an act of reassurance. You smile back, an act of reassurance. You say or do something aggressive. In response, she says or does something submissive, aggressive or reassuring. The ball's in your court.

If she's aggressive it may be a test of your courage and worth or she might be frightened and need to be reassured you intend no harm, then again, she may want you to drop dead. Reluctance requires more aggression. How much? Depends. Read on.

If she's submissive don't respond with aggression. It's been established, at least for the moment, you're the dominant one. Show you won't hurt or embarrass her by being briefly submissive, a smile, a bit of boyish awkwardness. Then be aggressive. If she reassured you, do the same.

How aggressive? Depends. On what? Your ability to determine what's needed for acceptance as dominant without chasing her away. How long will it take to learn that? Depends. On what? How good you are, right now, with women. Of course you'll have to scare off a few and get dismissed by several others for being too passive before you figure out what not to do. About fifty of each will do it!

WHERE SHE'S COMING FROM

When approached, her fears are the same as any female's. She doesn't want to be attacked or groped.

Once her primary concern is satisfied, she's afraid of the same things you are: being used, humiliated or rejected during courtship. She has her pride, just as you do. She can't respond directly to your advances without risking rejection by you.

She knows she can attract boys but doubts her ability to attract a man. You may be the first man, except for obvious dirty old men, to show interest in her and she's not sure it's real. She's in unfamiliar territory. The rules of courtship as she knows them may not apply. You could just be flirting with her. If she comes back with openness and receptivity you might laugh at her for taking you seriously. She cannot respond directly until she's feeling more confident in her ability to handle you.

Her defenses are up. She's extremely nervous and will take flight, physically or emotionally, if she experiences any of this as too dangerous. This as an encounter with a far more powerful male than she's used to dealing with. She's unsure of her ability to manipulate you. Will the ploys she uses with boys work on a man? She's doesn't know what she must do to avoid being dismissed as unworthy, thinking she's way overmatched. Appreciate how powerless she feels.

There's a thin line between being a powerful male and too powerful for her. The less confidence she has, the less power you show while remaining powerful.

To understand her emotional state even more clearly, realize she thinks your age and experience will enable you to charm her pants off before she wants them off. Add the element of self judgment. She may find herself guilty of perversion for being interested in someone old enough to be her father.

Directing and controlling her desire for you is an ever present fear of the consequences. For you, the worst that can happen is your friends and the rest of society, excluding your company, will cluck their tongues, smirk and say something like, "Ole Don Boy's trying to prove he's still got it." She's the one who will be chastised, ostracized, criticized or any other "sized" you care to name.

The younger, the more concerned she is about not looking perverted by showing interest in front of her peers. She must maintain her image, whatever she thinks it is, when they're around.

And now, the good news. She loves the novelty and excitement of flirting and being the object of a man's attention. If you don't scare her away she wants more, more, more.

RELUCTANCE, RESISTANCE AND TESTS

Young women don't respect or like you if you take any of their shit. They see it as a sign of weakness and an indication they already have you by the balls, just like their boyfriends.

She wants to know, "Is this guy a real man, or what?" She has to convince herself you're worth it. You must pass her "entrance" exams. These begin when she pretends not to be interested. She's testing your sincerity. If you persist, mildly, she's convinced. In the same conversation or the next, she rejects you gently, seeing how you'll handle it. If you get angry she figures she's already got you, the end. You also fail when you act hurt, like a little baby boy. You have to react like a man, the one described in *The Right Attitude*. She doesn't want another boy, she wants a man, even if it is scary.

When you fail her exams, you don't gain entrance, to her.

It's necessary to show interest but not too much, certainly not to the point of giving her control. You have to maintain the appearance of aloofness, otherwise she'll get around to you when she's done with everyone who doesn't chase her.

Rejecting you strongly is her way of avoiding a situation she can't handle or you came on too strong. Then again, she may think you're a dick. It happens. Keep my batting average of .190 in mind.

PRESSURE OR PERSISTENCE

If she feels pressure she will dig in her heels and you will be far worse off than if you'd just waited until you "accidentally" crossed her path again. Determine if you're doing it right by checking your inner state. If you feel like you'll die if you don't get to go out with her, you're doing it wrong.

You must really feel, believe and know with all you're heart and soul you can do just fine without her. That, my friend, is the state you'll eventually achieve if, and only if, you learn from your mistakes. After ruining it enough times you'll realize life goes on no matter which one turns you down. True enough, you'll feel like dog shit. It passes.

Later, when you've screwed up enough times, a light will come on in your head. You'll see young women can come and go without it killing you or making life a paradise. Achieving this state was a five year process for me. It still slips away, now and then. Don't panic in your second or third year.

LESSONS IN PERSISTENCE AND MORE. I met Kim, a sharp looking, slightly chubby (my favorite) six-foot blond when she was sitting with a woman friend of mine at a local restaurant. I joined them for a leisurely dinner. Good, good vibrations.

My friend went to the rest room getting ready to go home. I took the opportunity to suggest lunch to Kim, asked for her number and offered my card. She said she'd call me if it seemed like a good idea when she wasn't so tipsy. I was stunned. She was at least 23, old enough to have been here several times before.

She didn't call. I told my friend what happened, "Don' know, said she liked you, isn't dating anyone." I gave her my card, asked she give it to Kim and say I wanted to hear from her. Friday night she called. We chatted and made a date for Sunday brunch. I asked why she did not call before, "I had to be sure you really wanted to go out with me. You did."

During brunch it was obvious we were not on the same wavelength. To quote her directly, "I'm tired of getting screwed and lied to. I want to date one guy who only wants to date me." *Translation:* "I'm 26, going on 27. Desperate, gotta get married." I brought this on with, "I like to get to know someone slowly."

Lesson one: Persistence pays. She knows you're sincerely interested. Lesson two: Never married's over 25 are focused only on one thing. Want a clue? It's not having fun and enjoying the benefits of an older lover.

PATIENCE DURING COURTSHIP

"A bush or two in the hand is worth any bird."

The Author

I'm not a patient person by birth, upbringing or habit. I've learned by trial and error, mostly error, I must have patience to date young women. It was easy to figure out. I just watched one sweet thing after another walk away, not call, lie about why she didn't show up and "forget" dates. The younger she is, the more patient you must be. Even after all these years my impatience causes me to make fatal mistakes.

If you didn't meet at a party where you knew some of the young people in attendance or weren't introduced by a mutual friend, prepare yourself for a two-month or longer siege, depending on her maturity. That's if you can put yourself in front of her three times a week.

It takes time for her to get used to the idea of having an older lover. She has to resolve her feelings of guilt, then stop doubting her sanity. After that, she must accept the risks and generate the courage to take a chance. At the same time she's making sure you're not just going to use her then trash her. And finally, when she's gotten over the pervading feeling of "There's something wrong with me for wanting to go out with someone old enough to be my father," she'll accept a pseudo date.

This is not something that happens overnight, next week or next month. This takes time, energy, effort, money and patience.

THE GODS WILL TEST YOU. The other-world of young women is ruled by gods with a perverse sense of humor and bizarre timing. They severely test every older man who dares enter their kingdom, lest he prove unworthy to partake of the delights offered by the young females in their domain.

These gods have devised a particularly cruel trial for you after you're slim and trim, dressed well and dating a 28 year old. The pricks will wait until you're engrossed in the sports page on Monday morning at the coffee shop. Then they'll send a pretty, well endowed 19 year old to sit down beside you.

Prove your worthiness by reacting appropriately. Make this your touchstone: "Start out easy, you can always come on hard." If you startle her, radiate lust or even momentarily embarrass her during the crucial opening moments, all is lost. Make only a friendly, relaxed move. Smile and say, "Hi." Resist the urge to take charge. This was the hardest thing for me to master.

Don't get me wrong. There are times when she'll be most excited and interested by your direct, strong approach. However, you will make few, if any, fatal mistakes by waiting to see if coming on hard is what's really needed. When she's under 25, coming on hard is right only three times out of a hundred.

PATIENCE PREVENTS RAPO. Rapo, as in rape, is a game females of all ages play to avoid the dangers of intimacy, not sexual intimacy but emotional closeness. It is described best in Berne's, *The Games People Play*. I've been had by them all, from 14 to 40. Immature ones, of any age, play the most.

She talks and flirts with you, giving the impression you should make a move, now. You do. She recoils in horror, exclaiming, "What kind of girl do you think I am?" or the equivalent. You'll hear this equivalent a few (thousand) times, "I can't, I have a boyfriend."

She wants to know she's attractive and prove it to the world. By rejecting you in front of others she's saying, "Look everybody, he made a pass at me. I must be attractive." At the same time she wants to show the boys in the audience she's not a bad little girl. She's marriable, not interested in men. She thinks her actions translate to, "Look boys! I'm a good girl. I chased that bad old man away."

Okay. Here's another of those worth-the-price-of-the-book tips. Identify a Rapo player by how smooth, calm and relaxed she is during her interaction with you. She's not afraid. She knows it's only a game. Compare her with the typical excited, nervous, awkward, anxious 20 year olds you court. If it's too good to be true, it ain't.

A STRING OF PEARLS MAKES YOU PATIENT.
Always have a string to work on at least three young pearls long. With only two, when you "fold 'em" with the first, you'll only have one, that's the same as having none.

The more of them you're working on at once, the less likely you are to come on too strong. Your attitude will radiate, "If it doesn't happen here I can move on." You will be perceived as confident, relaxed, not desperate for a date with her.

When focusing on only one, for you, the stakes are high. She feels the pressure and would rather fold than stick around to see your hand.

Young women come and go out of your life instantly. She is unstable, impulsive and irresponsible. She is quick to get married, engaged or hook a boyfriend. New boyfriends don't get cheated on for a year. She's interested in immediate change when something is wrong. She quits her job after two frustrating days. She changes apartments, roommates and phone numbers faster than you change your socks.

Just after you managed to talk with her three days in a row down by the pool and then had her over for a drink last night, she decides, "Debbie and I are moving to Oregon. We want to get out of the smog, live a natural life." Puke!

Keep the hopper full. Have at least three, more if you can handle it gracefully. I can't. As one disappears, get another going. Keeping your options open is good business, no matter what business you're in.

IT'S AN ACT - SHE'S NOT A WOMAN
The young women you'll be dating lack the ability and confidence to relate to you like a woman can. They don't have much experience with older men and

a series of successful encounters to make them believe they can handle you. Most pretend to be confident and mature, assuming you won't be interested if she acts her age.

She'll have you believing, "No problem. She does this all the time. I can make my move now. She'll handle it like a woman."

Treating her like a woman means trying to take shortcuts. You assume she's not afraid, based on her behavior. You don't take your time and maintain the mandatory, casual indifference needed for her to think the affair is her idea. Dropping the pretense, you communicate directly, trying for too much, too soon.

You won't even realize you scared her. To save face, she'll control herself and continue acting like a woman until you're gone, then lose control, of her bladder.

Besides pissing in her panties, she'll tell the other girls where she works or where you both work, you came on to her. It serves two purposes. She wants to know if you're a notorious playboy and she wants all the other females to be jealous.

FUCK UP'S FROM THE REAL WORLD. Let's start with my classic. I rate it at the top out of, oh, probably a thousand.

Shelly was 21. She was physically, spiritually and mentally everything I find mega attractive in any female, young or not. She had a sharp mind. She was brave and strong. She was conscientious, ambitious and educated. Her absurd, silly sense of humor was backed by a grand, toothy smile and sparkling, devilish blue eyes.

Physically she was delightful. I don't know how to get this across, it sounds weird, but she looked like she'd burst through her skin. I think she was so full of energy and life it just looked like that. It's not important. It turned me on.

In the beginning I did everything right. I was sitting in the bar at a restaurant I frequented, bullshitting with a few of the girls who worked there. It was Shelly's first night as cocktail waitress. I ignored her. Her friend Debby was in visiting, giving moral support and having a few.

I engaged Debby in a conversation about Hawaii. The two of them were going when they graduated from Cal State in a few months. Shelly joined the conversation when she heard me discussing cheap places to stay. They asked tons of questions. I volunteered to bring in the information on state cabins. "When do you work?" Pretty slick, eh?

I waited four days. I sat at the bar and casually went over the cabins and suggested some hikes around there, then ignored her, had another and left. A week later I saw her car in the parking lot as I was driving by. Whoa! Suddenly it was Miller time.

On my way to the bar she stopped me, excited and happy, bubbling about getting reservations and thanking me for saving her so much money. I said, "No problem. You're a waitress too, huh. I'll sit with you next time I'm having dinner. Later."

How did I know her car, you ask. I'd bent the conversation that way the first time we talked. Pretty slick, eh?

Three days later I was working on a mild buzz, flirting with Sue, the bartender. I knew Shelly's schedule, didn't expect to see her, but she bounced in, bounced over and plopped down beside me. She had on tight blue jeans, tight t-shirt and no bra. Jeeesus, had I underestimated. Great medium large tits, great curvaceous hips, great legs, great, just fuckin' great. The buzz, you know.

I bought, we talked, Hawaii, backgammon, her trouble with advanced accounting, my inability with math, sorority snobs, and, tah dah, our mutual dislike of the bar scene.

The booze was working on us both. Soon she was telling great "dirty" jokes and laughing at mine. Her signals were subdued but definitely positive.

My little head started yammering, *"Shit. She's ready. Just lay this on her, 'Let's see if you're as good at backgammon as you say. We can go to my place.' She'll go for it. You can suck the nipples right off those tits. Let me fuck her doggie style. You can watch that big ass jiggle."*

My big head regained control when she left "to powder my nose." I knew I should say something tactful to test the progress and her interest. Remembering past mistakes I just said, in an "oh by the way" manner, I thought she was attractive. She blushed slightly, "You're not bad yourself."

I went to the men's room to get a hold of myself, both ways. I knew one more drink and I'd blow this opportunity before she blew me. After finding out her schedule as a waitress I promised to come in and have dinner when she was working, then said I had to go. Pretty slick, eh?

On the way home and for the next two days, I thought about her constantly, focusing on important things, like what those tits would look like flopping up and down while I was ramming her. Should I go down on her right away? Were her pubes dark blond or brown? I'll bet she likes being on top!

She ceased being a 21 year old, living at home, finishing college. I decided, "She's pretty mature, just too inexperienced to initiate it. She's only needs a tactful invitation. No need to wait. I'll have to be relaxed and sure of myself, though."

Thursday night finally arrived. I dressed sharply and threw down a couple to make sure I was "confident." When I got there I was feeling so "confident" I forgot to see where Shelly was coming from. I was so "confident" I started off the conversation, after amenities, by inviting her to come over to my place after work and beat me at backgammon! Pretty slick, eh?

She tactfully declined with a semi-plausible excuse of finals coming up and having to study. I was so "confident" I didn't realize I had just blown it. After days of fantasizing she was a woman, not a 21 year old. So I persisted. "We can keep it short. I'll just beat you three straight. You'll be home by midnight." She said, "No, really. I gotta study," and left with my order.

I knew she liked me. "Damn! She was so happy to

see me when I came in. What the hell's wrong? Maybe I'm not 'confident' enough." So, I had another confidence builder.

I was so "confident" I couldn't see the right call was to drop back and quick kick. It was early in the first quarter. But to my "confident" way of thinking I was on this woman's, not young woman's, one yard line. "So what if it's only the first quarter. You gotta score when you're this close. Power it in. Fullback over left tackle, on two."

You know what happened, right? I dropped the snap, then booted the ball. Shelly picked it up and walked, not ran, the length of the field for a touchdown.

Wanna hear the fumble? "Look Shelly, we don't have to play these useless singles' bar games. I'm attracted to you, you're attracted to me. Come on over." She turned pale and walked away. Another girl brought my check.

A month passed. I was sitting in a coffee shop. Shelly walked in, saw me, came over to my booth and sat down. She smiled that big toothy grin, "What you been up to?" I controlled my excitement and managed with great will power to be casual. We talked for awhile. The vibes were kinda good, so I figured, "What the hell, can't blow it any worse from here," and suggested lunch. She hesitated, then declined with no excuse. I figured, "What the hell, I'm not going to make it with her. Let's find out what the score really is." So I said, "Why not?"

Shelly looked me right in the eyes and said, "You're too smooth for me." I asked what that meant. Her reply, in effect, was she liked me, thought I was attractive but, "You're just trying to fuck me and I don't appreciate it one bit."

I figured, "What the hell, it's truth telling time." I said indeed, I wanted to "go to bed" with her but that wasn't all I wanted. I told her truthfully how wonderful I thought she was, how I'd love going places and having fun together.

She listened thoughtfully. I waited. The gist of her

reply: That fateful night, she had proudly told another waitress I was coming in to have dinner at her station. That dear girl said I was a slut, always trying to pick up the waitresses.

I remained calm with great effort. I told her it was not true. Sure I was friendly and flirted but I'd never asked any of them out. (I hadn't.) I wanted to know who had said these things, suggesting names of those I considered the cattiest. She wouldn't tell me. It made no difference, irreparable damage had been done by my "confidence." We parted diplomatically.

Somehow I had made a deadly enemy at that place without ever knowing it. Or, the girl who called me a slut was one of those cunts (I can name call, too.) who can't stand it when another female is successful.

I quit going to that bar-restaurant. Since then I've been extra careful not to flirt seriously with any waitresses, bartenders or cocktail girls at my other hangouts. Who knows when another, as dynamite as Shelly, will start working there. I'll wait. When she does, I won't forget she's not a woman, no matter what fantasies I have about her.

MORE FUCK UP'S. HEY, THAT'S HOW YOU LEARN. I met Sandy where she worked. After a few visits and several friendly conversations, the weather, UCLA versus USC, my recent trip to Hawaii and others, she invited me to lunch. "Here's one of those rare but wonderful adult 19 year olds. We won't have to 'dance' long," I thought!

A few days later on the way to the restaurant I asked if she had trouble getting served. When she said yes, I "cleverly" suggested we stop by my house and have a Margarita. She agreed. At that point I "knew" I was dealing with a 19 year old, capital W, woman.

Sound familiar? Don't feel bad when you're a slow learner. This was six months after Shelly!

We talked about college, her job and other safe subjects. I had another drink and "cleverly" maneuvered the conversation to relationships. Remember now, I'd talked with this young woman for a total of about one hour before getting her to my place.

She seemed comfortable with the topic. She said her 22 year old boyfriend was her dream lover and considered him "the 'man' I'm going to marry when I graduate." I talked about my ex and she had another drink. I had another drink and "cleverly" managed to bring up sex. Again, she seemed comfortable and talked about her somewhat recent loss of virginity, diplomatically emphasizing how patient and understanding he had been for six months. We had another drink and went to the restaurant.

"Patient and understanding," Nah, I didn't wanna hear that. I was three tequilas into it.

We talked and drank some more. The vibes were great. I was so excited and aroused by Sandy's maturity. After four tequilas I felt rich, handsome and sexy. I said, "You know what I want?" She looked at me sensually, leaned forward, revealing D-cup cleavage and in her best Cosmo Girl impersonation said, "No. What do you want?" Her tone of voice added, "You big, strong, powerful man."

Now I felt bullet proof! In my best Cary Grant impersonation, "I'd like to have a torrid affair with you." She responded, "I'd like you to take me home," as any 19 year old would.

When you screw up like this take heart. At least once a year I still I hear myself saying, "You've done it again, asshole!" right after she gets angry or scared and walks out of my life. Sometimes it's on the fourth or fifth date. I've decided "the time has come," ignoring my mandate to wait until she thinks it's her idea. I forget about having patience and start behaving like she's an adult woman. Always and forever WRONG!

Patience is not a virtue, it's mandatory.

WHAT ELSE CAN GO WRONG, GO WRONG, GO WRONG, GO WRONG?

Once you've mastered the basics you're not usually the problem. It takes time for her to get used to the idea of being interested in an older man. A week to her is like two months to us. Although she sees you as an interesting possibility in her life, her attention span is limited.

Fate intervenes no matter how patient you are. Old boyfriends come home from college or the service, her neurotic parents get separated or she meets Mr. Rite, where he works at the pizza parlor.

Remember Mr. Rite and his two outstanding qualities, marriable and marriable? If she doesn't have a boyfriend she wants one. She'll forget about you and "go for it" when a candidate appears, any candidate.

Things only go wrong at the right time, destroying months of preparation. It's just like the rest of your life, nothing except what you do is controllable. Everything else is up to the gods.

AFTER YOU'RE GETTING GOOD AT IT,   THE GODS TAKE OVER. You'll have done everything correctly. You'll have met her and after several weeks of "getting to know you" talk, she's happy and excited to see you when you come in.

You'll have mentioned something about fishing and she'll have said, "Gee, I always wanted to go fishing but Jimmy'd never take me." You'll not have jumped on that but two days later you'll have casually mentioned you're going pier fishing on Wednesday (knowing it's her day off) with Mary, a friend of yours and an acquaintance of hers (a built-in Teddy). She'll have smiled and coyly asked you to take her along. On Monday night she'll tell you excitedly she and Jimmy are going to Europe for the summer, leaving Wednesday. Typical.

Who knows what'll happen while they're over there or even more important, when she gets back. If you pout about the fishing expedition or indicate anything but happiness for her, you'll have no chance. You've spent so much energy developing this, work on saving it. A long shot is better than no shot.

Handle it like a man. Give her your interesting card. Write your home address on the back. Ask her to send you a post card. Then mention some of the places you think she and Jimmy'll like without trying to one up him.

Another - What Went Wrong? She was 21, a solid B plus. You met her on Tuesday, shook her hand, smiled and talked for a bit, then parted. On Thursday she remembered you and smiled. You talked some more and told her you'd see her on Monday. She said, "Okay, have a nice weekend." Monday, she wasn't there. You knew better than to ask. Today, Tuesday, you didn't notice she wasn't paying attention to you. You were excited, started talking. She barely replied. You left feeling like a jerk. What happened?

Review her last few days to get a rough idea what her world is like and how that world, as well as fate intervene in the best laid plans of mice and middle aged men. She has pressures, people pulling and pushing on her all the time:

(1) Yesterday she skipped work to take her best friend to the abortion clinic so the girl's parents wouldn't find out. Her boss said this morning he'd fire her if she missed another day.

(2) An hour after she went to bed last night her old high school boyfriend called again, crying and begging for a chance to make it work, threatening to kill himself. He's a coke fiend.

(3) This morning, Tuesday, she was 20 minutes late for work. Her car wouldn't start. She called her boyfriend. He wanted a blow job as he drove her to work and got "totally mad" when she wouldn't do it.

(4) Last night her girl friend was trying to convince her to lie to Jimmy so they could go to Palm Springs this weekend. She's considering it after the way he was this morning.

(5) Her never-married older sister always wants her to baby sit. When she says no, as she did ten minutes before you walked in, her sister makes her feel guilty.

Yeah, it's an exaggeration. But all of these and many, many more have happened to young women I've been courting or dating. If only one of these things happens, you're not real important to her, today. Take heart. Don't quit. Go back on Thursday or Friday and give it another shot. Patience, perseverance and tenacity are virtues necessary to prevail.

Understanding her universe won't make it much easier to date her. But when things fall apart, knowing what she may be going through will give you the courage to try with her again.

Sometimes The Gods Have Nothing To Do With It. When she tells you not to do something, don't do it. The telling is not done directly. You have to pay attention, then remember.

Early on after meeting Janice, she told me she was bored shitless with her live-in boyfriend of three years. "But," she confessed, "I don't have the balls to really cheat on him." I sympathized and kept my mouth shut. A few months went by and we became good friends. She excitedly told me she had gotten up the courage and was going to go out with a guy from her work. A week later I asked about her "date." Angrily she related the first time was great, "I wore his cock off." But two days later he brought her flowers and told her he'd found the love of his life. She said, "I told him I was living with someone. I just wanted to mess around. The dick."

Now this young woman was "hot stuff" by my standards. She was 20, had a great sense of humor, was good looking, rowdy, rebellious and loved to party. I lusted for her but was being patient, waiting for Janice to realize I was just what she needed.

A month later she said, under the influence of champagne, "I'm ready to fuck my brains out, going crazy. How 'bout Wednesday night?" Patience is rarely honored that directly, okay.

Wednesday night finally arrived. I handed her a rose when she walked in. She didn't say anything except, "Thanks," then asked for a drink. I took my time and waited. After an hour she said, "Sorry. I just want to be friends, okay?"

In the three long days I had to anticipate the wild delights of this luscious young woman my brain must have quit working. She had told me how not to behave two months ago. Handing her a rose was like slapping her in the face and saying, "What are you doing here with an old man? You should be home, loyally waiting for your faithful, boring boyfriend." If you missed in reading, what I missed in the real world, read it again then keep your ears open when you get out there.

COURTING TACTICS

The most dangerous enemy you face is from within: your lack of confidence, your too confident, too aggressive manner, your lack of aggression. These are tough to overcome, even with practice, so the best general strategy is to be unpredictable, swinging between being nice and being coldly indifferent. It keeps her off balance and enables you to maintain an effective perspective on the relationship. Without the right viewpoint, you are liable to be wrapped around her 22 year old finger in a couple of days.

When you're obvious or up front about wanting to go out with her there's no longer a challenge or the excitement of not knowing if you'll make a move or not. Besides that, she's scared. So, when she's certain about your interest, she convinces herself the outcome is so obvious she doesn't have to take any chances and even make a pseudo date with you.

This entire enterprise is complex but it's not that much different from the prancing and dancing we have to go perform with some adult woman. Young ones like to mind fuck, too.

Pay attention to the signals she's sending you. From all the body language books you'll know what's going on most of the time. But, if it feels like she's coming on to you, even when there's nothing concrete you can point to as evidence, she is. That's what courtship is all about.

Some young women are blatant in their come on's. There is no mistaking what's happening. But be suspicious of her if she's relaxed and smooth. Even when it seems like she's really inviting you to make your move, it may be nothing more than bait to get you in position to rebuff your advance and win the little game of Rapo she's playing.

DIFFERENT WORKS. She has an unlimited choice of males, relatively speaking. So here you are standing in a very long line, trying to have an affair with her. If you compete with young males using their weapons, you'll never get to the front of the queue.

You can't be like the young competition except in one important way, you must be young at heart. During the courtship you must show her you are exactly that, young at heart. You run four miles a day and enjoy physical, outdoor sports. You like to play games, have fun, laugh, be silly and party. She does not want to have an affair with a serious, tired, jaded man.

New is exciting but you want her to see you're not only new, you're radically different. The only chance you have is by being different. Different looking. Different acting. Different talking. Different in what you want from her.

When talking and interacting with her don't make sexual comments, he does. Don't talk about how great you are, he does. Let manners and etiquette show, he doesn't or doesn't know how. Don't try to impress her, he does. At the same time, let her see you have attributes and knowledge she'll benefit from in the near future. When it fits, always mention some of the things you like to do a young man doesn't do: attend plays, go the horse races or drive to Beverly Hills for Sunday brunch at an elegant restaurant.

Don't, that's Don't with a capital D, say or do any of these things to impress her. If she even slightly suspects you're trying, it ruins everything. She thinks she's got you.

You're from a different world. She wants to find out what your world's like. But, everything must be done carefully. Different is exciting but also dangerous. You don't want her to think she's not mature enough or smart enough or whatever enough, to explore a different world. Present your world so she knows nothing adults do will embarrass her. It will be fun, exciting and different. Different works.

THE COURTSHIP PROCESS IN ACTION

I went to the supermarket and replenished my liquor supply. I looked over the cashiers and got in the line with the best looking one. Her name tag said, "Liz."

She smiled and gave the standard Alpha Beta greeting. I volunteered it was a week's supply, got no response except a polite smile, so I shut up and watched her ringing up the booze. When she got to the Cuervo Gold she said, "Now here's something worthwhile!" with a happy grin. Without thinking I told her I loved it in sunrises but didn't shoot it like "real men." She laughed and said she did. After some small talk about tequila I told her I'd be back to see her next week when I ran out. She laughed again and said, "Okay."

I went to the store the next few nights but she was never there. Then one evening I had a date with Lisa. She wanted Kamikazes and nothing but Kamikazes. I gallantly went to the store, alone, for lime juice.

Liz was working! I grabbed the limes and a fifth of Gold. I pushed the Cuervo forward without saying anything. She looked up and smiled, "Finished the big one already?" I said, "Nope. I bought this one to drink with some wild and crazy young checker I met." She looked at the clock, looked at the tequila, then at me, "Not tonight. But sometime soon." I smiled and said, "You've got a date," and left to down Lisa and a few Kamikazes.

Liz was never there when I went back night after night. After a week I asked. She had been transferred to a store a few miles away. I changed supermarkets.

She noticed me in her line and looked around nervously. I got the hint. When it was my turn I was all business. She was frightened but glad to see me. I asked her when she worked. She hurriedly said, "All different hours, the holidays." She kept watching the checkers on both sides while ringing up my stuff. I kept quiet, said good bye pleasantly and left.

I went back many times during the next week, she was never there. I lost my patience and asked the manager when Liz worked. He gave me a suspicious look and said he couldn't give out information like that. Oops! Too pushy. Time to be patient.

Two weeks later I was sitting in the lounge of a local dinner house after a blacked out Laker game on satellite. Liz walked in, still wearing her uniform. I waited. She never looked around, just kept her eyes glued to the tv.

When a commercial came on, I walked over and said, "Hi, Liz." She didn't smile, didn't say anything and looked scared to death. I realized she didn't recognize me so I asked if I could buy her a Gold shooter. She grinned a big smile of recognition, "Sure!" slid over and patted the seat beside her.

After amenities I told her a short version of what happened when I went looking for her. I explained I didn't want to ask many questions at her new store because I didn't "know her situation." She thanked me for that and said she had been on vacation.

After another drink she shyly volunteered she never went to bars and certainly would never let a man buy her a drink. I was smart enough to just wait. Within a minute she "confessed" she was angry with her boyfriend and didn't want to go home until he left for work on the midnight shift.

After some safe small talk and another shooter she said, "Sorry I was nervous when you came in." Before I could say anything she added, "Ed's sister was working the register behind you." I didn't have to ask who Ed was. My cock stiffened. I mumbled, "Uh huh."

We made some awkward small talk, then I asked, "When can you come over and work on that fifth of Gold with me?" We made the arrangements for two nights later. She said she'd have to leave at 2 am because he sometimes called on his first break. (Remember Many Ann's and Jimmy's checkup calls?)

Twenty minutes after she came through the door we were in bed. We had a passionate, two month affair. It ended when she started feeling too guilty.

Let's review this courtship effort from the beginning and see why it worked.

I was ready, as always, for the first meeting, clean and dressed neatly. I put myself directly in front of her. I didn't keep trying after getting no response to my attempt at conversation. I waited, aloof and indifferent. When she did say something I replied with information about me.

I could have ruined it right off when I resorted to humor but that's the real, spontaneous me. I was able to reply as I did having written off my chances when I got nothing but a businesslike response after I had given her the perfect opening. In other words, I really was aloof.

We both were able to indicate interest without risking rejection, as shown by the way I closed the first conversation with a pseudo offer for a date and got a pseudo yes.

I was tenacious, going back until I found her. Then, was confident, relaxed and aggressive, suggesting we drink together, and got at least a "sometime soon." Was confident and aggressive again, saying, "You've got a date."

Knowing I was going home to face certain orgasmic death at Lisa's delightful hand made it easy to be confident and relaxed when making the proposition.

The deal I offered Liz was safe, no one had to lose face since either or both of us could pretend it wasn't a "real" pass if she wasn't interested but she knew I was strongly attracted. It wasn't "Let's have lunch sometime."

Her reply, "sometime soon," was safe for both of us, too. It could mean "maybe," or it could mean, "Not tonight, but soon, we'll drink a bottle of Cuervo and see what happens." The whole exchange was instinctive. I just did it and so did she. Nobody can plan ahead how or what to say and pull it off.

Sometimes when I hear "maybe" or a version of it I react negatively with fatal results even if she meant "possibly" instead of "Stuff it, jerk," which is usually what "maybe" means.

My negative reaction takes the form of attempted face saving words, followed by defeated body language and facial expression. After that she writes me off as a wimp even if she was only: (1) stalling for time because I rattled her (2) seeing if I was sincerely interested by waiting for me to try harder or (3) testing the steel content of my balls. Confident men are indifferent or positive when responding to "maybe." I was confident. It was easy that time, Lisa was waiting.

From the beginning I was careful to be discreet. When she was nervous at the new store, I did nothing and said nothing that would cause her fellow checkers to notice me. And, after creating suspicion in her manager's mind, I stopped going to the store. When I told her about that in the bar I chose my words carefully to imply I wanted her, boyfriend or not, "I didn't know her situation." And, we could have pretended I meant her work situation if either of us needed to save face.

Having her walk into my life was not all luck. She chose the dinner house because young people don't look for each other there. She didn't want to be seen by any of her contemporaries. I was there because I only operate a few miles from home and never, never hangout where young people on the make go.

Notice the phrasing of, "When can you come over and work on that fifth of Gold with me?" Confident men assume it's "when" not "will you?" The time and the vibes were right for an aggressive, confident move.

Liz was ready for an affair but was so attractive she could pick and choose. She wanted someone safe. "Safe" meant someone knowledgeable enough not to get her discovered, someone who understood her situation and accepted it, as well as someone she could keep emotional distance from and who would not behave like a jealous boy.

After *Boyfriends* you know most have one. Assume the one you're courting does and let her know it's cool. Endangering her relationship guarantees you, not she, will be the person washing your cock real fast in the shower.

Liz, and all others who don't hangout in bars, wanted someone who didn't just want to pop her once or twice and drop her, making her feel like a piece of meat. I had shown genuine, sustained interest in her. I met her requirements for a safe affair by demonstrating discretion on several occasions. And, I behaved like a confident, relaxed man who was attractive enough. I was slim and trim, and dressed well. Preparation met opportunity.

SUMMARY - THE ELEVEN COMMANDMENTS OF COURTSHIP

Dost thou covet thy neighbor's young ass? Verily I say unto thee, to gaineth such, thou hast but obey the commandments of courtship:

I. *Thou shalt have a slim trim body*
II. *Thou shalt be well groomed*
III. *Thou shalt be dressed right*
IV. *Thou shalt smell good.*
V. *Thou shalt be relaxed and confident*
VI. *Thou shalt shake hands and smile*
VII. *Thou shalt talk at her level*
VIII. *Thou shalt radiate no lust*
IX. *Thou shalt laugh appropriately.*
X. *Thou shalt remain adult*
XI. *Thou shalt genuinely compliment, once.*

One through four are mandatory. No discussion. Five is the hardest. Don't despair. A moderately well acted imitation will work until success permits you to be genuinely relaxed and confident. With only a bit of practice six is easy. The seventh only forbids attempting to impress.

Breaking *VIII* is fatal 85 percent of the time. *VIII(a)* is: Thou shalt steal no glances at those perky tits.

If you're into macho nine will be hard to obey. Drop the Clint Eastwood act. Laughing at yourself is even better. Ten simply forbids acting young and hip. Eleven is hard for introverts. You are simply asked to focus on her, what she has on or looks like. Zero in on one thing you sincerely admire and tell her. Not that great tush, either. Notice it says "once." In *Meet Her* and *Talk With Her*, there's much more about why.

Mastering one through five will have you dating her less than a year after finishing this "bible." After you're able to obey them all, Hefner will come to you for lessons. Seriously, these commandments are no different from the original ten. You can't observe every one.

Relax. Only one through four are absolute. Just get moderately adept with three or four of the others.

Verily, brother, woe be unto thee, if thou doest not obey the first commandment. Thy present world and thy hereafter shalt be inhabited with only fat, ball crushing divorcees of two score years.

So, you know what you have to do to get ready, you understand her and have the basics needed to court her. Let's see where and how you *Find Her.*

"When hunting ducks,
one must go where the ducks are."

Field Marshall Rommel

Find Her

While you get fatter watching the tv newsman tell
you about another kid dying of leukemia visiting
Disneyland, another wreck on the freeway, another
arson fire in the garment district, another benefit for
AIDS "victims," another day of your life goes down
the drain.

There are thousands of young women out there
right now, within five miles of your place. Several of
them would be delighted to have an affair with you.

No matter what it says in *How To Pick Up Girls*,
finding her and meeting her are different but inter-
twined steps. The only practical place to find her is
where you will have a semi-plausible reason to say
something to her and then have a safe subject to talk
about.

You could go jogging at the high school when the
senior girls gym class is on the track. I used to when
married. Jesus, it was marvelous being passed by fifty
giggling 18 year olds. They smelled so good. It was
delightful watching their titties bouncing. But it's
absolutely of no use. Mommy told her, "Don't talk to
strangers!" I told you, "The only practical place to
find her is where you will have a semi-plausible . . ."
Remember it.

WHERE TO LOOK

Any place she is not trying to meet a boy or young
man. Find her working in restaurants, bar-restaurants,
offices, shops, stores. Look for her in classrooms,
campus organizations, female-type classes, resorts,
vacation spots, tennis courts, health spas, parties,
weddings, issue clubs, political clubs and participating

in community charity events like End Hunger Walk-athons.

In 1988 there will be 8.7 million females between 18 and 21 in the country. Six million will be enrolled in colleges or other educational institutions. What are you doing sitting here reading a book. Get your ass into a university or community college class room.

Whoa! Come back here. Take a shower and put on some nice clothes and expensive cologne. Run that razor over your face. Be confident of your appearance. Don't let her first impression of you be that of a scruffy, middle aged man. The ten minutes this takes is worth every second because there's no such thing as luck, only preparation meeting . . . .

Pick a class with interaction, not one where you get lectured to. I met at least 40 potential young lovers my first semester on a junior college campus. I dated three. One became the life-long friend mentioned before.

WHERE NOT TO LOOK

Any place she's trying to meet a young man. Anywhere the crowd is mostly under 25. In a class like Investing in Krugerrands. In your living room watching Monday Night Football. Any seminar on How to Meet People. Any pop psychology workshops or any gathering for singles. Never look in any bar, especially a singles' bar.

WHY NOT SINGLES' BARS? Most divorced men and women, and many who never married, end up behaving like the young males of our culture. Well, at least the people looking to meet someone for the night or the rest of their life, in a bar.

You were a young male. Remember when you were 22? You'd say anything, do anything, just to get laid. That's how the single world is. It's populated by desperate, defensive, manipulative, game playing liars of both sexes.

Everyone's blowing smoke up everybody else's ass. Nobody wants to get hurt, again. Experience teaches them all, "Do unto others, before they do unto you."

Singles' bars are the worst possible places to look

for her. When she's on the prowl she's focused on finding someone three to seven years older. She won't even notice you. If you are stupid enough to approach her, you will get shot down rudely. She's trying to impress "him," so she publicly embarrasses you.

If she isn't trying to meet someone, her reasons for going to a bar are to: test her powers of attraction, practice talking with males in her age range, satisfy her curiosity about bars, enjoy being looked at, prove to her girl friends she can attract males, play Rapo for her own enjoyment as well as her friends' entertainment, get away from her boyfriend, pretend she's grown up or just dance.

Besides having motives that don't match yours, her anxiety level is off the scale. Some of it is created by the general tension in the air at these meet-to-meat markets but most of it comes from her own fears of being rejected or humiliated or, the ultimate failure, no guy even makes a pass. Her defenses are stronger than a case-hardened chastity belt.

She's not experienced enough to realize most men believe a girl is in a bar to meet men. She's genuinely offended when you "hit on" her. Her indignant reply is never pleasant, often humiliating.

If this isn't enough to make you look elsewhere, let me tell you what happens even when you are doing well with one of them. When it comes time to close the sale (phone number, go elsewhere) she realizes what's really happening. "My God, I've been picked up by an older man, in a bar!" The shock causes her to mumble something about taking her girl friend home, then she bolts for the door. Or, she gives you her number and then bolts for the door.

When calling her a few days later my experiences include hearing, "Gee. I'm really sorry. I didn't mean to give you the wrong impression but, I had a fight with my boyfriend that night, we're back together." Or, "I was drunk and didn't realize what I was saying." Or, "You were so persistent I didn't know what else to do." The most humiliating was calling what I thought was her number and getting Dial-A-Prayer!

Even Weber himself, wouldn't try, *"That dimple on your . . ."* in one of these places. He's got a "sure-fire" line for singles' bars though. I saved it for the next chapter, *Meet Her.*

God does work in wondrous and mysterious ways, his miracles to perform. You may find her among all the plastic losers. I, however, am of little faith. After wasting a year of my after-divorce life I only learned the one I want is not in any bar. Save your money and your ego, skip this part of my education.

GET READY TO FIND HER

Get out of that nice safe rut. Get away from those nice safe "friends." Get up off your ass and do something. Don't wait for it to happen. Make it happen. Think. For example, riding stables are full of young mares. I hate horses, otherwise I'd try it. If you're neutral or like horses get going, she's there.

Visit the library. Talk to the Research Librarian and have her help you list all local clubs and organizations. Pick the ones you think people under 30 would join, Young Nazis for Social Change or the equivalent. Join ten. Go to a meeting. Drop the ones you were wrong about. Try these for sure: Society for the Prevention of Cruelty to Animals, Green Peace, Sierra Club, Young Republicans, Young Democrats.

Join the ski, hiking or any other club at work. Become a member or manager of the company's softball, bowling or whatever team.

There are plenty of young waitresses within 15 minutes of your home or office. Don't go to eat when the crowd's there. Get there earlier or later if you want her to become interested.

Limit your hunting grounds to an area you can cover quickly and often. Stick close to home and work. You have to be in front of her as often as possible, like every day, to meet her. More important, most under 22 are reluctant to drive more than 20 minutes to your place, distance is intimidating to them.

Once you've established a small circle of young friends and acquaintances, throw a party for any reason. Invite them all. Tell them to bring friends. Pay for everything.

Break a leg or visit someone daily who's hospitalized. You'll find ten Candy Stripers and young nurses.

Take night or day classes at the local junior college interesting to females between 18 and 30. She's in Sewing for Beginners, Acting I, Word Processing, Paralegal Training and such. Read the listing of classes and figure it out. Take classes at the local YMCA or even better, at the YWCA.

Get your hair and nails done every week by a student at the local beauty college. Not by one of the fags, of course.

Go to the beach every day. Become a "local." After the sun goes down, hang out in the restaurant/bar where the under 35 crowd goes. Beach town bars are different. They're like, you know, dude, really kicked back, casual to the max.

Rent a house at the beach right on the sand for two weeks or longer. Sit on the front steps and get to know the local young men. Drink beer with them. Sooner or later young women will appear.

Summer resorts are the place to be if you don't live near a beach. Get a cabin situated so you can sit on the steps and get to know the young men who spend their summers there. Drink beer with them and just like at a beach house, the young women will soon appear.

At a resort town like Palm Springs, get there early Friday. Situate yourself so late arriving women have to walk past you as they check in. On Saturday afternoon use the same techniques described in *Meet Her* for weddings. For those methods to work you must have broken the ice once before with a low level, non-threatening, subtle, friendly first move. Saying "Hi," to her on Friday when she walks past you is just that.

Get invited to every wedding, any wedding, anywhere, anytime. No matter how old the bride or groom is, young women will be everywhere. If you have steel balls, crash, rather, wander in to any reception after it's been going for an hour.

FINDING HER AT A WEDDING

Since there is a wide range of ages among the guests, you blend in. This makes sending and receiving signals of interest possible without causing her problems.

Catty competitiveness is rampant. Females of all ages are envious of the Queen for a Day. If you're slim and trim, and dressed well (you'd better be) some of the girls, at least half the young women, more than half the women and some of the older women will have an eye on you.

Keep a low profile until the signs of interest have been exchanged. Narrow the field to one or two and make your move.

No matter what you do you will be talked about, prejudged and watched closely. This is the price you pay for not "knowing your place," which is going home to weed the yard. But no, you're going to smoke weed, with a 21 year old bridesmaid, in the limo's back seat.

FINDING HER AT YOUR WORK

Your office building is a prime hunting ground but most of us have seen the consequences and high cost of personal involvements at work. You may prefer to not risk your position and future even for that 20 year old centerfold working over in Accounting.

If you have steel balls and brain power, you can ignore the unwritten rule of not dipping your pen in the company ink well. I do, and did, and will, as you will see. Discretion is mandatory on her part as well as yours. You can count on yours but you'll never know about her until the heat is on. Proceed accordingly.

Focus on the young women who are employed by some other corporation if you work in a large multi-tenant building. Use the young friends you've made at your company to find and meet the young women working for one of the other companies.

To find and meet a young woman on your own who works on a different floor or for another company, you'll have to "bump" into her several times or be lucky enough to be in the right place at the right time, and by now, you know what Lombardi and I think about getting lucky.

Get up off your ass and go down to the snack shop several times each day. Sit there. Sip your coffee and read the paper with an eye on the door. Most of them are creatures of habit. Go ten minutes later every day until you spot her, then be there each day until you can figure out how to meet her.

Be pleasant and say "Hi," when you "bump" into her from day to day. Gradually she will start to feel like she knows you, after that you'll be able to strike up a conversation when "preparation meets opportunity."

Keep everything casual except for a few brief, moderately intense glances. Until you're sure she's interested, show no obvious interest in her other than just friendship. In other words, don't stare at her and don't look at her ass with lust in your eyes as she's leaving. Her friends will be watching you.

After you've exchanged "Hi's" for a few days, time your return to the elevator to coincide with hers, without being obvious. It's easier to talk to her before the elevator arrives. Once inside, she's even more frightened because there's no place to run away from a potential dirty old man. If you do it right a few times you can drink your morning coffee with her as a first pseudo date.

FINDING HER AT YOUR NEW COMPANY

Remember what I told you way back there in *Get Ready For Her* about changing companies? Here's why. I was working for a company with 3000 employees, now I'm working where there are only 400. One reason I changed was the high percentage of young women at the new place. There were many more at the old job but few were in my building on the 100 acre complex.

Now, they are all in the same building, not more than 300 feet from my desk and I have to "bump" into them all day, every day. I am only smiling and saying "Hi" as I pass each of them in the hall or any other place, and at the same time, I am taking inventory and noticing which ones are friendly and extroverted. This is just the second week and I've identified three potential candidates.

As yet I don't know which ones are truly available but I know two are interested, based on body language and eye contact. I am taking my time. I want to pick a winner, not a cock tease. Everyone knows everyone. When I make my move, the rest will find out then lose interest or cause problems.

This week I am joining the slow pitch softball team and soon will be drinking beer with the younger males after the games. After a couple of weeks I'll be invited to a party where I'll be able to meet and talk with all the females easily. However, since some young women from the company will be there, I'll only engage in mild flirting, otherwise, "He's a slut," will get back to the office and my chances of picking one from the many disappears forever.

Besides meeting young women at the party, I will meet young men who don't work for the company. I will hit it off with one or more of them and will eventually be included in their circles, where I will meet more young women, with the added advantage of no girls from work to cause problems.

As you can tell, finding a young woman through work and friends is my favorite and primary method. It's relaxed and natural to find, meet and then talk with her at a friend's house or even just sitting out by the pool. She's not defensive or playing games like she is when looking for Mr. Rite in a bar.

When you've finally gotten yourself into this ideal situation and you're ready in every other way, some of the young ones will be wondering what it's like to sit on your face. They don't want you to know, so keep it casual. Patience is mandatory!

NO NO'S WHILE LOOKING

Don't look lustfully at the girls working in the coffee shop where you're becoming a regular. Don't do it at your new company either. They are all watching and checking you out, too.

Looking at more than one with drool on your chin makes you a very dirty old man. Looking at only one like this causes the others to tease her, so she ignores you even if things had begun. You must be above suspicion. Talking to one about liking another causes the same thing to happen.

PICKING AND CHOOSING

Remember the advice I gave you a hundred pages ago: (1) Forget high schoolers, disco dollies and born agains, as well as big titted girls and beauty queens, the competition is stiff. (2) Go where the competition is limp, stick with 6.5's to 8.0's, they're better human beings and more fun. If she's Miss Teen-Age Anaheim, packing a pair of 36 DD's, wearing a $75 hair cut, with a dove around her neck you won't bother, right?

Should you be lucky enough to have a choice between three 20 year olds, all equally interested, you will be smart enough to choose the 7.3 not the 8.7 or the 9.2 won't you?

When more than one is showing interest, be patient. The smooth one's probably a game player. If they're about the same age, pick the one who shows the most genuine interest after a couple of hours. If they're all showing the same level of interest and one is 19, one is a typical 20 year old and the third is 23. Pick the oldest. The chance she is on the pill, driving her own car and living away from home is a hundred times greater.

It requires four times as much patience to get an affair started with a 19 year old as it does with a 23 year old. Once it starts, the young one needs two days to set up the subterfuge necessary to come over for an afternoon. She has a boyfriend, and a mother, and a father, and a brother, and a nosy girl friend and she can't spend the night. The 23 year old comes over anytime her boyfriend can be bullshitted.

Did you get that back there at the beginning of this chapter about finding her only where you have a reason to say something. I hope so, otherwise you'll have to get a new copy of *How To Pick Up Girls*, and use one of those "trusty" lines to *Meet Her*.

"So if you happen to be in one of these singles' bars some crowded Friday night, and you see a girl you dig, don't hesitate. Don't knock yourself out thinking up a witty approach. All you have to say is, 'Hi, how ya doin'.'"

Eric Weber, author, *How to Pick Up Girls*

Meet Her

Gimme a break. Do you suppose the putz really believes that? Christ I hope so. May he try it every Friday night for the rest of his life. It might work if you're Robert Redford, otherwise I submit, disrespectfully, there isn't any 40 year old man who can walk up to any 20 year old woman and get anywhere with any opening line.

In the past ten years I've never been able to date a young woman I met in some other way than being introduced by a mutual friend, she introduced herself or I introduced myself at: a social gathering, a class, a club meeting, my company or her work place after frequenting it as a customer for weeks. But then I never tried just strolling up and saying "That dimple ·on your left knee is absolutely sensational!" Tiny testicles, I guess.

The purpose of meeting her is to talk with her long enough for her to *". . . realize you are: (1) safe (2) interesting and (3) attractive."* I hope that sounds familiar.

When you're introduced the hard part's over. There's nothing left to do except talk with her but that's the next chapter. This one's about meeting her all by your little ole self.

AT YOUR OFFICE

Acknowledge her existence with a friendly "Hi" as you go by her desk or pass in the corridors. Non-verbally let her know you're slightly interested but not dying to meet her. You're becoming familiar, not a stranger. "Hi's" are first conversations, making second ones easier.

Do this as often as possible without being obvious for a week or so. You're looking for any sign of interest on her part, a smile or "Hi" in return, plus the ever reliable good vibes.

"How's it goin'?" from her is great. But don't stop and talk with her now. Reply on the same level based on your personality. Mine is, "Oh 'bout C plus, working on a B." Tomorrow or, even better, the day after, go back and, under any pretext, preferably business related say something, "Hi. I'm looking for Jim Fulkerson's office. Do you know where it is?"

If she tells you, fine. If she doesn't know, fine. Your response is similar. "Thanks," or, "Oh well. I'll find him." Then extend your hand, "I'm Don, work over in data processing." She'll shake and tell you her name. Don't chat long, move on, you're only slightly interested.

I noticed Suzanne, 22, walking to her car in the parking lot and in the cafeteria. I had smiled and said "Hi" when passing her in the hall on several occasions. She and some co-workers were bullshitting in the aisle when I was on my way to the third floor to see Gus.

I stopped and said to all three, "I can't find my way out of this maze. Where's the stairway to the cafeteria?" Suzanne said, "Follow me." On the way I introduced myself and shook her hand. She reciprocated. We exchanged small talk. Two days later I "had to" see to Gus again. On the way, I went past her cubicle and said "Hi." On the way out I stopped and chatted briefly. You know, where I worked, the dumb shits in purchasing. Two chats later we made a lunch date.

I run a sports betting pool at every opportunity. It gives me a reason to introduce myself and to talk with her by trying to sell her a square or a team. Later, I go back with a progress report or to let her know who won the "big bucks" and talk about how close she came to winning it all.

WHERE SHE WORKS

She's where you have some reason to talk to her: waitress, store clerk, librarian. Do the same things you do at your office. It takes longer and coming up with something to say is harder. Keep putting yourself in front of her over and over. It makes her feel she knows you. It's easier for her to talk with you if you're not a complete stranger.

Gina, 20, was the morning cashier at a coffee shop near my office. I had been going there for a month and although we'd only exchanged amenities my eyes had said "What a tush. I'd love to eat you." Her eyes had said, "Maybe." I met her by saying, "Jesus, am I hung over," to her usual, "How y'doin t'day?" She gave me some aspirins from her purse and commiserated, relating she had one Friday.

The next morning she asked if I'd recovered. We talked about drinking. I suggested we have one together. Two days later we met for a Margarita when she got off at three. She was not subtle. After asking how old I was she laughed and changed the subject abruptly. With one more drink she confided she'd lusted after a 50 year old at her dad's company when she was 16. We lasted nine weeks.

WEDDING RECEPTION OR PARTY

The process is the same but compressed. She's going to be gone in a couple of hours. You must start faster, build faster and think of something to say faster.

Start faster by saying a friendly "Hi" to each and every person you see from the time you park the car until you're situated where you can look for her. You're building a foundation to work from. This gives you the chance to say later, "Hi. Saw you on the way in. I'm Don. Work with Jim," or friend of the bride or went to school with Sally.

Build faster by using this line to introduce yourself and have conversations with as many different people as possible. You're setting it up to meet her. Keep it short and move on. The more people you meet the better your chances are. It makes no difference what sex or how old.

When you see her talking with one of these people you'll be able to join their conversation much easier. In fact, you might even get introduced. And, it's easier for any of the sweet young things interested in you to join a group you're in. They know the people you're talking to. In fact, you might even get introduced. Got it?

Acknowledge her anytime you have the chance. Say "Hi," nod and smile on your way to or from the rest room, bar, kitchen, pool. You're just being friendly. Remember, these "Hi's" are first conversations. It's the same as passing her desk at work or being her customer day in and day out. You won't be a stranger when you start the second conversation.

THE PHOTOGRAPHER PLOY. I stumbled on this one when volunteering to take informal shots at a friend's wedding. Females love to have their picture taken, period, no matter how much they protest.

Take a camera to parties and weddings. Don't be an obvious ass and only take photos of the girls. Shoot lots of pictures of everyone. It gives you a chance to meet and talk with even more guests.

When a young woman's in a shot ask her, "Would you like to get copies of these?" Depending on her reply you have options.

Her response, including tone of voice and body language, translates to "Jam it, old man." You say, "Jim'll have them, probably Saturday if you change your mind." (Adios, bitch.)

If she radiates moderate interest with her words and non-verbal signals you say, "They'll probably be done, Wednesday. (Smile, offer your hand.) I'm Don, friend of the bride." When you shake hands, her vibrations will let you know if you tell her (Adios, bitch) or if you say what's just below, when the signals are positive.

She replies, "Sure!" and her sparkling eyes say, "Gee, you're kinda cute." You say, "Let's fuck!" Not drifting off, right?

Okay. You really say the same thing, "They'll probably be done, Wednesday. (Smile, offer your hand.) I'm Don, friend of the bride." As you shake hands notice if her vibrations match what you think she said without words. When they do, respond with, "Nice to meet you Debbie. I work in Anaheim, live in over in Torrance," and wait. You just put the ball in her court.

Sometimes she's so new at this she doesn't notice the ball come over the net. Sometimes she's seeing if you're nuts are as big as you're mouth. Sometimes you're so excited you don't see her Daddy standing there. Like a chess game, after a couple of moves the options are endless.

In the name of optimism let's pretend she says, "Oh yeah? I live in Fullerton." Hand her your interesting business card, say, "Here's my number. Call me at work. I'll meet you somewhere with them on Thursday or whenever. Okay?" Leave. Go back in a half an hour. Talk with her. Dance with her. See what "develops." Yuk, yuk.

THE DO-YOU-KNOW-HIM GAMBIT. Here's another wonderful method I discovered by accident. Situate yourself where you can confidentially say to her, "Do you know that bald guy's name? I've met him, can't remember. Don't want to embarrass myself." If she does know or doesn't, thank her, introduce yourself, shake hands, talk briefly, then move on to the bald guy. Part with, "Wish me luck." See, just like at the office. Move on now, come back later.

I've used this to get her to notice me and as an opener after signs of interest from her. You can't lose. It's innocent looking and sounding. She feels empathy. Everyone's forgotten somebody's name. You have a face saving exit if necessary, leaving to talk to the bald guy. And, you have the perfect excuse talk with her again. She's wonders how it went with the bald guy, so you go back and report, right? It works at any gathering, wet or dry but wait awhile if people are drinking, booze loosens her up and stiffens your spine.

CLASS OR CLUB MEETING

The principles are the same as meeting her at your office. She's going to be there, so go slow. Let her know you're aware of her existence and acknowledge it. Just say "Hi" and not much else. Don't appear to be anything but friendly and slightly interested. Be discreet in front of anyone else.

Let her become used to you. Get to know other people first. She'll feel less threatened if three or four people are going to the student union for coffee at break or to the restaurant-bar after the meeting.

Get on the same subcommittee or student project without being blatantly noticeable. When the situation is right, under any pretext, ideally class or club related, start the second conversation. Remember to shake her hand and introduce yourself a few minutes into it.

YOUR ATTITUDE WHEN MEETING HER

This sound familiar? She's drawn by indifference, feigned or real. You're friendly, not dangerous and somewhat interested, aloof but possible, if she plays her cards right. "I am the catch here, not you. I'm not going to chase you."

WHAT TO DO WHEN MEETING HER

When introduced or when introducing yourself extend your hand, shake her hand firmly, look her in the eyes and smile. Be alive. Laugh and relax. Serious is not attractive to the young.

In California people under 25 are on a first name basis. I don't know about elsewhere but here it's uncool to ask for or use a last name early on. I don't like it. I conform.

After a few minutes of talk, compliment her on anything you genuinely like or admire about her, especially her clothing and accessories, not her great tits. This has to be real or you're dismissed as a bullshit artist. Praising something she chose, like a bracelet or her shoes is the best. Everybody tells her she has beautiful eyes. You're different. Only one compliment per conversation though, you're only mildly interested.

ON SHAKING HANDS. Shaking her hand makes you different from the boys and young men who nod and smile when meeting her. She instantly knows you're in another category, "Men."

A ton of real data is exchanged as you two touch for these three seconds. What you learn is gut knowing. She can't bullshit your stomach and you're a fool to ignore it's judgement of her. Look into her eyes and, for a few seconds, be vulnerable. Let her see you. See into her. It confirms or denies your other impressions of her. If you know what she's really like, as opposed to what she appears to be, you're way ahead of any competition around. You can adjust your courtship approach and pace accordingly.

Although some of the younger ones are a bit disoriented when you offer your hand, they quickly recover and reciprocate. Sometimes it's in a submissive manner, sometimes as a sexual equal, sometimes as the opening move in a game of Rapo and sometimes like a dead-pussied bore.

I've saved myself far more than the price of a drink by excusing myself at the earliest opportunity after shaking hands with some of them. I'm not interested in game players or teases. One sophisticated looking beauty turned out to be nothing but a shy, frightened doe. Not my type at all. On two occasions I was able to skip ninety percent of Phase One preliminaries based only on the sparks that flew when we grasped each other in this socially acceptable manner.

Carla told me, a month into our affair, she had been quite impressed, "I felt so ladylike." Not one was ever repelled.

THE TEN COMMANDMENTS OF MEETING

Show her how discreet you are from the beginning. Never make moves on her in front of her peers or anyone else for that matter, no matter how much champagne she's got in her. Don't come on so lowkey or so aloof and distant she finds you cold and uninteresting. You absolutely cannot be stuffy. Read these commandments slowly. Think about all the implications

of each one. These are not like the *Eleven Command-*
ments of Courtship. You can't break even one of
these.

I.   *Thou shalt not stare at her tits or ass*
II.   *Thou shalt not mention the ex or children*
III.   *Thou shalt not look at other females*
IV.   *Thou shalt not talk over or down to her*
V.   *Thou shalt not be slick and smooth*
VI.   *Thou shalt not be negative or cynical*
VII.   *Thou shalt not mention sex*
VIII.   *Thou shalt not ask about boyfriends*
IX.   *Thou shalt not touch, except to shake hands*
X.   *Thou shalt not indicate standing interest in her*

FOR THOSE OF YOU WITH STEEL BALLS

To meet a really good looking one, remember she's
being "hit on" all the time. She's so used to flattery
the man or boy who compliments her makes no impact. She's bored with the same old shit when someone's trying to pick her up. She has no respect left
for them. They try so hard or kiss her ass.

Use a different approach, one that rattles her
confidence and causes doubt of her lofty status. Tell
her she has the ugliest shoes you've ever seen and
walk away. The next time you go back you'll have her
attention. Play it by ear. Your only chance is to blast
her and shake up her defenses so you can penetrate
them, and her, later. You have nothing to lose.

It doesn't have to be shoes, it could be an ugly
ring, hair piece, anything that's out of place. Don't
criticize anything she can't change, her nose, her
fingers.

It won't do any good to say, "You're so pretty, but
you ruin it all with those ugly shoes." To the point.
"Jesus! Those are ugly shoes."

You know how to find her and meet her. But you've
only just begun. We homo sapiens conduct our court-
ships with conversations. It's time to *Talk With Her.*

*"Once negotiations begin,
it's only a matter of time
before castle walls crumble
or maidenhead breached."*

Churchill

*"When a girl says yes,
she means maybe. When she
says no, she means yes.
When she says maybe, she means no."*

Single Male, explaining "them"
to the author circa '79

Talk With Her

The first conversation is only to show her you're safe and interesting. (A second, but important purpose is to make certain she isn't a SWAT team member's girl friend.) Your goal in all subsequent conversations is to let her see you're an attractive, discreet man, someone it would be fun to have and affair with.

WALK A MILE IN HER SHOES

You're 20 years old, make $5 an hour and live at home. The world you live in revolves around friends, college and partying. Your oldest friend is 24. Self esteem is derived from your car, your clothes, how "cool" your friends think you are and your girl friend's appearance.

Seven different girls have been out with you, the oldest was 20. You got hand jobs from four, French kisses and titty squeezes from all and "did it" with three. One was Rosy Roundheels, the other two were steady girl friends.

You have no idea what you'll be doing a week from now, let alone two months from now. In the back of your mind you plan to marry before reaching 30.

You're a couple of beers into it at a gathering

where there are people of all ages, say a wedding reception. Three of your buddies are standing right over there, just to the left of the table where your uptight parents are sitting. Your girl friend's about 20 feet away, dancing with her brother. A somewhat attractive woman of 40 extends her hand, introduces herself and starts talking with you. How do you want the woman to behave in this situation? Got the picture?

At 20 years of age you want the same things from her as the young woman you approach wants from you: (1) Don't be pushy, I'm not good at telling people to buzz off. (2) Don't be obvious, although I may be interested, I don't want everyone in the room to know. (3) Realize I'm scared, I've never done this before and even if it's exciting, I see you as very powerful and dangerous. Jeez, you're a grown-up. (4) Be casual, friendly and relaxed, it'll help me stay that way. Don't show you're nervous, it makes me nervous. (5) Keep the conversation superficial, further into it, leave a few openings for me to tactfully indicate how we're doing and if I want to continue or not. (6) Later on, when I'm more sure of myself, don't ask for too much. Give me room to maneuver to save face, mine and yours. (7) Don't act like an asshole if I turn you down, you started this.

ON NOT BEING DIRECT

All young adults communicate obliquely during the early phases of courtship. If you're straightforward it throws off her timing as well as disorienting her, and makes her feel you're not playing by the rules. Forget the "communication skills" you learned from your marriage counselor or therapist. They are completely ineffective in the single world.

At a minimum, direct talk makes her think you're out of it, or crazy. After a few dates when you're comfortable with each other, you can gradually start being more to the point, but in the beginning, indirect exchange of information is the only way to fly.

Single people are not direct for two reasons: it protects them from the humiliation of rejection if the other person isn't interested and, indirectness makes it possible to use the other person without risk of involvement.

Everyone is a suspected game player. She's trying to protect herself. Hey, too bad, that's how it really is. I didn't make the rule everybody's playing by: All's fair in love and war.

DYNAMICS OF FIRST CONVERSATIONS

In the game of backgammon, opening moves are so crucial the outcome is often decided in thirty seconds. It's the same in this game. When you do and say the right things in the critical first moments, the moments to turn into minutes. The longer you sustain contact, the easier it is for her to see you're safe, then interesting. Only after that, can she find you attractive.

Once she's decided you're not a threat, she checks you out physically. If you're slim and trim, dressed well and don't break any of the *Ten Commandments of Meeting*, three minutes later she's deciding if you're a playboy. If you've done nothing and said nothing to lead her to believe that, she's wondering what you'd be like in bed and considering it.

She's had few opportunities to be picked up by an older man who wasn't an obvious dirty old man. After a few minutes she knows that's exactly what you're trying to do. But, she's wondering why you're talking to her. She is confused, not realizing how attractive and exciting she is to a man.

As you interact emotional vibes and signals are exchanged. The longer you talk the better, up to a point. Five minutes into the first conversation, it's time to move on, for awhile. Remember, to strongly attract her you must have the right attitude. Demonstrate you're only slightly interested by walking away.

ONLY WHEN SHE'S INTERESTED

Either you say something or she does. If she says something first it's nearly impossible to mess up.

I've learned to go first only when she's shown interest, a smile, sustained eye contact, "accidently" touching me, preening after looking my way, breaking her eye contact by looking down instead of away, facing me with her body while talking with someone else, et al. Read your body language books, you'll know when she's considering a mustache ride.

A few moments after you see she's interested, and only after she's interested, get your ass over there and say something before you talk yourself out of it. I start thinking about all the bad things that could happen, then all the reasons she isn't that attractive, why the other one's more interested, bla, bla, bla. If I "Just Do It" and don't think, analyze or worry, it gets done.

OPENING LINES

There's a knock at the door. You're not expecting anyone. You answer it and find a smiling, well dressed young man with a briefcase. He opens the screen door and hands you a brochure, spewing, "Hi. I'm Dick Brain. We're conducting a survey in your neighbo.." You cut him off, "Not interested," and close the door. The boy had no chance with you, a man who's heard bullshit openings many times before, right?

For Christ's sake don't use one of those "clever" Disco Dick lines from the bar scene, "Want to come over to my place and look at the ceiling?" Something like that confirms her darkest suspicions of older men and you.

What's your name? What's your major? Do you come here often? Haven't I seen you somewhere before? That dimple on your left knee! You're a Scorpio? Those are high school and college boy lines. You're a man. Show her the difference from the git go.

She wants something different from a man. She certainly doesn't want you to be obvious. She wants you to be graceful and oblique. Say something that can only be taken as friendly but casual interest in her as a human being.

REAL WORLD EXAMPLES. Sonia, 19, assistant, city library, after good eye contact on three occasions across a week. I asked her to her run my card through computer, pretending I couldn't remember if I'd brought all the books back. She had a college sweat shirt on. "You going to Cal State Fullerton, Library Science? I went there, English. Easy, you know."

Donna, 18, coffee shop cashier, after good eye contact on a daily basis for two weeks. She had Rolling Stones decals and bumper stickers all over her VW. As I paid my bill, "Saw your stickers. I'm a Stones fan. Couldn't make the coliseum concert. Had to work. D'you go?"

Angie, 24, print clerk at a company in the same building as me, after good eye contact over a week's time. She was in the personnel office hiring in the same day I did. "Hi. We started the same day last week. (Offering my hand.) I'm Don. How do you like it so far?"

Jean, 18, girl at a wedding reception, after good eye contact over an hour and noticing her listening in on some of my conversations. I butted into one of hers, "Get all the student grants you can. Lie on the application if you have to. You'll pay it all back to the bastards in taxes after you graduate."

Suzie, 22, accounting clerk at a company, after great eye contact over two weeks in the cafeteria. She was sitting "accidentally" two tables away looking at me. I looked right at her and bit my apple like I was eating her. She laughed. I walked up to her in the parking lot after work. "Hi. (Offering my hand.) I'm Don. I'd like to meet you."

Kerri, 22, day waitress, at the bar as a customer one evening after serving me a few days before. "You're really a good looking woman when you don't have on that stupid uniform."

Deanne, 21, computer programmer at a company, after good eye contact and a smile from her the day before. I was driving to another building and saw her walking but talked myself out of stopping. She was coming up the steps as I was leaving. "You walked over here in that heat? I was going to stop but figured you must'a been going to 207. Sorry."

Margie, 19, girl at mixed age party, mild eye contact from time to time. I was working on a buzz, waiting in the kitchen for her to come near me. "Hi. I'm Mike's volley ball friend. (Offering my hand.) Don. You work at his office?" The buzz provided the courage, by the way.

Start it off differently. Keep it going by staying different. Different works.

TALKING WITH HER THE FIRST TIME

If you're not formally introduced there are three kinds of first conversations, arranged easiest to impossible:

She'll be there tomorrow.
She'll be there for a few hours.
She'll be gone unless you say something.

I cover the first two. Buy another copy of Weber's book for sure-fire methods to pick up chicks anywhere.

Let's stay at the wedding reception where you walked a mile in her shoes, so you'll remember what she wants from you as you talk with her.

AFTER INTRODUCING YOURSELF. The first topic is how you and she know the bride or groom. You go first and tell her. If she doesn't reciprocate, say something like, "You know Sally from college?"

The young woman's cold!? Hey! You were supposed to be talking with her only if she showed interest in you. Go over to the bar, look in the mirror. See, your head's up your ass. From now on only talk with her if you two have exchanged signs of interest.

Okay, from the top. The first topic is how you and she know the bride or groom. You go first and tell her. If she doesn't reciprocate, say something like, "You know Sally from college?" This step is necessary. You have to help her get past these first few moments. Give her something she can handle easily, no matter how anxious she is.

It makes no difference what she says, you respond with information about yourself. "Oh yeah? I've known Sally for three years. She was on the same volley ball team as ole Roger, over there, and me. You play volley ball?"

She's just like the young woman whose picture you took, after the opening moves the options are infinite. The key is giving her information about you, so she'll feel free to give you information about her, then you'll have something to talk about.

You can say, "Nice reception, great band." Or, "Great weather we're having." It's safe, not helpful. These statements are useful when your brain freezes, as it will from time to time.

You have to defrost it quickly though and get back to revealing yourself. "Seen Road Warrior III? I liked it, but I kept saying to myself 'What's Tina Turner doing dressed up like that?'" Or, "Sally and Allan always come to my annual Raider Party. She doesn't like football but loves to party, me too. You like pro football?"

What do you do, right now, when talking with women the first time? This isn't much different once you get past the first minute by helping her. The key is revealing yourself first, then giving her the chance to do likewise, "You know Sally from college?" "You play volley ball?" "You like pro football?"

Only show your interest non-verbally so she can reply non-verbally, that way no one's afraid of being rejected.

Reveal yourself with safe topics: recent movies, television shows, colleges, drinking, parties, Hawaii, skiing, back packing, cars, sport teams, the beach weather, where you've been recently, or are about to go.

She's just like the girl you met at the office, you talk briefly, then move on. You're only slightly interested, right? Excuse yourself and go to the rest room, get a hold of yourself. Let the champagne loosen her up.

SECOND CONVERSATIONS AND BEYOND

At this reception come back for more after you wander around and make certain you're not missing anyone better. *Translation:* a few years older. Stop and talk to that stunning 35 year old in the red dress. Show the young women what they're up against, it makes them try harder. You may not even have to go back to the one you just left. Once she feels competitive she might come to you. Silly games, right? But oh so necessary.

The purpose of the second conversation . . . This is a test. Flip back to the first paragraph of this chapter if you don't remember. Okay, we're going to stay at the reception, first.

When you can weave it in without being obvious, disclose yourself as single and available, "When I got divorced, bla bla." "My ex-girl friend used to, bla bla."

Don't follow my advice blindly, follow your instincts. Remember back there in *Court Her* I mentioned being able to skip Phase One preliminaries based on a hand shake? If she wants to smoke a hooter in the parking lot three minutes into the second conversation, be discreet, but get on with it.

TACTICS. You have to show interest in her. Not strong, direct interest, as it makes her pants wet, the wrong way. Remember, casual. You're walking a thin edge here. Too much indifference makes her lose interest and quit trying, too much interest makes her hesitate from fear or makes her feel she's already got you. You want her to wonder and not be sure of herself.

Some feel that by just talking with you and being friendly they are chasing you. When you don't show some interest in her she's humiliated, the end. With others, once they see you're really interested, they write you off as a pushover. All this was explained in *The Right Attitude* and *Court Her*. When in doubt, re-read.

In general it's best to make her feel like she has to try harder to get you to make your move. It makes her shit or get off the pot and keeps her guessing, as well as thinking about you when you're not around. The best course to follow is showing brief flashes of intense sexual and romantic interest. Not with words, right? Separate these with long periods of being nice but relatively aloof. Be mean once in awhile. Throw in a few digs to irritate her, too. This upsets her balance and breaks her rhythm of engaging in, what she considers, harmless flirting.

The difference between talking with her and talking with a woman is, slow and easy's never wrong. With a woman it can be fatal.

Statements about yourself are best, followed by a question. But ask questions carefully. Don't seem nosy or trying to find out where she lives. You're a suspected child molester. She doesn't want you following her home, at least not yet. More about this delicate topic in a few paragraphs.

WHAT TO TALK ABOUT. Anything she's interested in. Not the new tax bill. Remember walking a mile in her shoes? Keep the topics superficial but show yourself, give her plenty of opportunities to reciprocate. That's what verbal intercourse is all about.

Reveal more of yourself in second and third conversations. What kind of music, cars, clothes, food, restaurants, et al you like. Later, or, even now, if the time is right, reveal what you like to do radically different from her boyfriend.

Talking about places you've been or are going is always good unless you come across as trying to impress her. If you're able to discuss it without trying to dazzle her with your world travels, it is a good, safe, useful topic.

She wants to travel. She has no money. Her boyfriend's idea of travel is going down to San Onofre and sleeping on the beach so he can surf early in the morning. You're a potential vehicle for visiting faraway places with strange sounding names.

As always, you go first to find out if she's geographically desirable, too. Delicately weave in where you live and which town you work in. Just like when you were talking with Debbie when she wanted a photo, you're putting the ball in her court. Giving you this info is solid evidence she's attracted to you, even if done in an "oh by the way manner." She knows it, now you know it.

Don't push this. Right now it's not important, so

don't blow it. If she reciprocates, great. If not, wait a few sentences or paragraphs. Don't put any pressure on. It can be done with grace and subtleness, "Is that a long drive from where you live?" after she mentions where she goes to college, or works or plays. If that didn't get it out of her, I wait a while, then my phrasing is "So which town do you live in?" but only when the time is right. "Where do you live?" is direct and makes her stumble, as well as feeling pressure. "You from around here?" is a bush league, boy's move, demonstrating strong interest too soon.

Keep talking. Keep revealing yourself. Listen for anything she says that makes it feasible to suggest future contact for any reason. In *Date Her*, the next chapter, you'll see just how to do this but right now let's focus on why you're talking with her.

At a wedding or party your primary goal is to have her want to talk with you again, somewhere, somehow, some way: the party you're throwing one week hence, Bruce's Ram-Raider bash Sunday night, lunch at the Charley Brown's a couple of miles from her office and yours on Tuesday. Endless semi-plausible reasons exist. Use your big head.

Your secondary goal is to get her away from here for any reason, a first date, so to speak. A run to the store for more booze, cigarettes, some coffee to sober up, a music tape from her car to get more people dancing. Caution. Don't try for too much too soon. This is a young woman, not a woman. Remember Shelly!

Let's suppose you can't come up with anything that's even semi-plausible. Further, let's assume the party is starting to fade along with your chances of setting up a third conversation and you're at least 60 percent certain she's interested in you. Now what? Well, my man, it's time for some steel balls. Discretely and I mean inconspicuously, hand her your interesting business card and say, "I've gotta get going. I enjoyed talking with you. Give me a call. Let's have a drink sometime soon." Then you must leave. The odds of her calling are 20 to 1, but a long shot is better than no shot.

Before getting into second conversations when she's going to be there tomorrow, and all other conversations, you need answers.

INEVITABLE QUESTIONS - ETHICAL ANSWERS

This is a recording. If getting laid is your motive, put on a wedding ring and act married or get a young hooker.

Do not lie! Tell the truth. If you lie she'll know. If she doesn't know, what the hell do you want with her? You're interested in having an affair with a nice young woman who likes you, not some dick you pretend to be.

The minute she starts asking these questions she's interested, attracted and considering what it would be like to have an older lover. The more of these she asks in any single meeting, the more interested she is. It usually takes five separate talks after the second conversation with her to get through all of these. Have your versions of my answers down pat. Notice it's arranged so what she asks is translated into what she means, likewise with your answers.

Debbie: How old are you? *[I'm interested in you.]* **You:** Two years older than Mick Jagger. *[Don't lie now. You'd go out with him wouldn't you?]*

Debbie: How old, really? *[If you're too old to marry me, I don't wanna waste time.* Possible second translation: *Jus' wanna know how old'a guy I'm goin' out with.]* **You:** Forty six, going on twenty seven. *[I'm young at heart. I don't lie, I tell the truth.]*

Debbie: Are you married? *[I hope not. This is looking better.]* **You:** Nope. Got divorced. You married? *[I know you're not but let's see how you handle this first pass. I'll decide where to go after finding out.]*

Debbie: Do you have any children? *[I hope not but I suppose you do. Damn, what'll they think of me?]* **You:** Uh huh, one. *[Here's a hard return to your back hand. Let's see what you do now.]*

Debbie: How old is he? *[Please God, don't let him be my age. Is he too old or too young to be a prob-*

lem if we date?] **You:** She's 17. *[I'm old enough to be your dad. So what?]*

Debbie: Does she live with you? *[I hope not. I don' wanna hafta meet her. Gawd, what would I say?]* **You:** She lives with her Mom and stays with me every other weekend. *[Ain't no problem babe.]*

Debbie: How long you been divorced? *[I'm not so dumb. I read* Cosmo. *Guys who just got divorced are trouble.]* **You:** Five years. *[Ain't no problem babe.]*

Debbie: Why'd you get divorced? *[This is looking pretty good. You aren't a drunk or anything are you?]* **You:** Oh, you know. We just couldn't get along. *[I'm kinda normal. Ain't no problem babe.]*

Debbie: Are you going to get married again? *[Are you one of those mid-life crazies I read about in* Cosmo?]* **You:** When I meet the right Girl. (Emphasis on Girl.) It's not that great being single. *[I'm okay. Not one of those crazies. I've gone through all that. And, I'm not breaking your bubble.]*

(If she sees you somewhere with a young woman or you've talked with her often enough for her to realize you date young women, this sequence takes place.)

Debbie: Was that your girl friend with you at the restaurant? *[I thought you were interested in me.]* **You:** Nope. Just a girl I date. I don't have a girl friend. Don't like 'em, gets too complicated, just like to have fun and enjoy life. *[Ain't no problem babe. Now you really know the score. Well? Let's get on with it.]*

Debbie: How old is she? *[She looked as young as me. Oh my Gawd! He really is interested in me.]* **You:** Denice is 19. *[Ain't no problem babe.]*

Debbie: Why do you date such young girls? *[I'd like to go out with you but isn't that sick?]* **You:** I like young Women. (Emphasis on Women.) *[Are you a Woman or just a little girl, afraid of a man?]*

Debbie: Why? *[I'm a little afraid, yes, but I might take a chance if you give me a good rationalization.]* **You:** They're just interested in having fun and enjoying life. They don't want to get married, right now.

[There's a good rationalization and now you really know what I'm offering. Watta you say babe?]

(Sometimes this next question comes up whether or not Debbie saw you out with a young woman. The remainder of the questions come up no matter what.)

Debbie: What if your daughter dated someone 46 years old? *[If it's not so sick will you let her do what I'm about to do? Pass this test, Jack!]* **You:** I raised her so she learned to make up her own mind about everything. She does whatever she wants. She's pretty smart. Doesn't do drugs. Doesn't drink and drive. I don't make rules for her. I think if my parents had done that with me I wouldn't have been so wild. *[It's not sick, okay?]*

Debbie: When are you going to get married again? *[Do you and I have a chance of ending up married?]* **You:** When I meet the right Girl. (Emphasis on Girl.) *[You may be the one. No promises. I'm not breaking your bubble. Let's get on with it. You're starting to sound like a 27 year old.]*

Debbie: What do you do? *[Are you rich?]* **You:** I'm in data processing. *[I'm not saying anything about bucks until you learn I'm not gonna be your sugar daddy.]*

Debbie: Do you have a girl friend? *[I hope not. Things get, like, you know, messed up, I'd feel like a home wrecker.]* **You:** Nope. Don't like 'em, gets too complicated, just like to have fun and enjoy life. *[Ain't no problem babe. Now you really know the score. Well? Let's get on with it.]*

Debbie: But, I have a boyfriend? *[Tell me it's okay to have a fling, please! It's not that bad to fool around a little, is it?]* **You:** I don't mind. *[Not only is it okay to have a fling, it's great. I'm no jealous boy. Ain't no problem babe.]*

When I've talked with her correctly before she starts asking these questions, my answers work about half the time. The rest of the time either I picked the wrong one or she doesn't like the truth. I won't lie. I want to have a caring, romantic affair with her because she likes me, the real me.

If you only want to get laid, call up one of those swinging singles you met on the way down the age ladder. That's all she wants, too. You don't need the horrendous complications brought on by lying, not to mention how little you'd think of yourself for using an innocent human being. She will be lied to soon enough but don't you be the one who makes her behave like a defensive, manipulative, angry, singles' bar fly. Let it come from Danny Manly, Randy Red-Porsche or Sammy SilverBeemer.

When you don't get anywhere, she didn't like the truth or you picked the wrong one or you need to re-work you answers. Don't start lying. Think about what you said. Think about what she was really asking. Figure out a way to keep your integrity with a re-worded answer.

Some version will work for you, half the time, once you learn from your mistakes. Do not lie. The reason you're doing all this is to date a young woman who likes you, not the man you pretend to be. If you bullshit her into dating you, it won't make you feel like a man. It will make you feel like a callous prick, which is what you are when you lie. She's out there. Patience and honesty will find her.

SECOND CONVERSATIONS AND BEYOND WHEN SHE'LL BE THERE TOMORROW

Connect with the first conversation by mentioning anything she said the first time. If she told you where she went to college, say you read in the sports page UC Santa Cruz is changing the name of it's team to the Fighting Banana Slugs. If she mentioned a concert she was going to, tell her you heard it was a sellout or the reviewer didn't like it or anything you know about her world. Get the subtle message in her head you've been thinking about her.

FORBIDDEN TOPICS. Never, absolutely never say "I'm never getting married again." Never volunteer that you're dating other females. Never knock marriage and children. Never be cynical about such things until much later in the affair, like a year.

Sex is verboten during the early conversations. Don't bring up the subject in any fashion. Don't swear for five conversations even when she says "fuck" every other word. You're different, remember.

Don't respond in kind to her sexual innuendos or "dirty" jokes. Change the subject without making her feel she committed a *faux pas*. Don't pretend you're offended as an attempt to be funny. She may think she did shock you. That'll embarrass her or make her think you're "out of it."

Deep down she believes talking or even joking about sex with someone she barely knows makes her a bad girl, especially when he's a grown-up. Although she wants to know she can attract a man it's too much for her to deal with sexuality, yours or hers, early in the courtship.

At the same time she's testing you to see if you're interested in her as a sex toy or if you really like her as a person. Pass the test.

After you two know each other, sex can be joked about, then discussed, tactfully at first and later, straightforwardly. But this is one early mistake you can never, and I mean never, recover from. It's always fatal. See "Foot In Mouth Stories" at the end of this chapter.

Don't belittle her beliefs, values or tastes. Keep your cynicism to yourself. Don't make fun of how young she is. Don't mention or even look at another female.

Fantasy, not reality is important. Talking about or explaining Supply Side Economics is certain to make her face reality.

Never ask how old she is. If you ask her, she'll ask you. It forces the age difference issue into the open. She does not want to admit she's 19. She likes pretending. Besides, young women perceive you as five or ten years younger if you're dressed right. Let fantasy prevail.

To anyone 20 years old, something more than seven years ago is ancient history. Viet Nam happened in the stone ages, and so did you, if you talk about the bad old days.

ALWAYS SAY. During each conversation genuinely compliment her once, and only once, especially on something others don't normally notice. Not her beautiful hair, not her beautiful eyes. Not her beautiful complexion. Maybe her teeth. But, if you can notice something that reveals her personal taste, she knows you're different, special. Her clothes, shoes, jewelry and accessories are the ways she makes a statement about herself.

DON'T ACT SUPERIOR. Don't act like a parent or teacher giving advice, it only emphasizes the age difference. If she asks for advice like she'd ask a good friend, carefully say what you think and talk with her as an equal. If she asks for advice indirectly, beg off or play dumb.

Coming across like someone vastly superior to her in knowledge makes her feel ignorant. Explain anything like it's simple and only a matter of looking it up or knowing where to look. You just happen to know this because you read about it or do it for a living or whatever. She could have known it, too.

Tactfully done, talking about something she's asked about or wants to learn about is dynamite. It clearly shows how much better off she'd be dating you in addition to her boyfriend, who's only interested in his car or how much beer he can drink at a party.

You want her to come away from learning something thinking, "Gee, he's the kinda guy I'd like go out with, learn how to scuba dive." As opposed to, "Wow, is he smart."

HUMOR IS DANGEROUS. Humor can be an ally when you use it to show you're not a serious old fart. Laughing at yourself is best. Being silly and joking around to poke fun at life and the absurdity of it all is pretty safe. But to attempt making a point with humor is often deadly.

She's concerned with how she's coming across, wondering if she's acting like a woman, unaware that you don't want a woman. She's so busy worrying, she usually misses the joke and, of course the point. Then, either she feels stupid or thinks you are. Fatal.

Joking about her figure, appearance, clothes, car or anything else about her is taking an unnecessary risk. Young people are so sensitive about their image and get their feelings hurt far more easily than old fools like you and me.

There is a fine line between being funny and being crude to a young female. Never attempt to be witty about sex. The girl who showed interest and was starting to become attracted, can, and will, suddenly write you off as a dirty old man if you offend her. You can ruin three hours of preliminaries with one sentence. You are a gentleman. This is a recording. You're different.

SETTING IT UP TO DATE HER. The set up includes disclosing you're single and available in the same manner you used during the second conversation at a party or wedding.

Other setups include thinking of some way she could do you a favor. Like asking if she knows anyone with a VW convertible for sale or if she sees one for sale to tell you. Anything to get her to think about you when you're not there.

I let her know I work on cars as a hobby. Perhaps a week later, or more, she might ask me why her car keeps stalling at lights. I can assume she's asking me out.

What can you do a young woman can't? Hook up car stereos and home stereos, video cassette recorders and other mysterious electronic devices? Can you do income tax returns? I can edit term papers. I rewrote one that led to a two and a half year affair. Can you get her a summer job where you work? Think. Make a list of what you can do before you meet her.

FIFTH CONVERSATIONS AND BEYOND

Continue revealing yourself, especially things you like to do she's never tried and her boyfriend's not interested in. Other than that, you only have to talk about topics of interest to her. It's not much different from a woman now that she's interested.

Sit down and write a slanted, interesting one page autobiography. Commit it to memory. She'll ask, probably after two conversations about you and your history. On the first real date, she'll want to know details, somewhat like a pedigree. Don't brag. Do say what you've accomplished that you're proud of.

Be ready to discuss your divorce honestly and without sadness or regret in your eyes, tone of voice or on your face. If you can't do this, you're not ready for young women no matter how ready you are in all other ways. It took me two years, 96 tears, 36 bouts with self pity and at least 26 ruined first dates with women under 30. Don't be afraid to say you've screwed up. It makes you a human being. Don't dwell on it and come across like a loser or a basket case.

HER MIXED UP HEAD, NOW. She believes in boy-friend-girl friend, Jimmy and Debbie together forever. But, she knows young couples who are cheating after only one year of marriage. She's seen acquaintances turn into blimps after one child and a year of daytime television. She knew a girl at college who "slept with" her English prof and wonders, now that you're in the picture, if it might be fun.

It takes time for her to realize she can have fun and learn something with you. If you try to be directly honest with her before you get to know her well, that is, until you've been to bed with her many times, you will fail. She doesn't know what to do with straight talk. It is a foreign language to her. She communicates obliquely and by implication, as most people do.

You can't rush it. She moves at the pace she feels comfortable with. You can't level with her. You can't talk sense, make her see what she's missing or you'll get, "Oh, fer sure, on 'Days of Our Lives' and stuff, older men have affairs with girls but, you know, I don' know. Gee, gotta go, pick up my brother. See ya."

Wait until she sees it for herself. She will, eventually, if you're patient and fun to talk with. Continue being yourself and acting like a man, not a boy, and she'll realize what she's missing. You're just being friendly and enjoyable until she sees the light. Then, when she does go out with you and realizes you're a fun date, you can relate to her like a 27 year old.

She's concerned with the moral rightness of dating you. She expresses it as a question, about why you date young women. You can prevent her asking this one by answering another. She leaves her mind open when she asks about your marriage and why it didn't work out.

PLANTING SEEDS. Sow this intellectual seed early in the courtship. Later you'll be able to plant your chromosome seeds. Even if I bumbled into it by accident, it's worth a $1000, plus the price of this book. Send your cashier's check to the address in *Closing Advice*.

I was honestly responding to a question about what happened to my first marriage. In a long rambling answer covering boredom, each of us changing across the years, ad nauseam, I said something like, "A couple of years after our divorce we were talking. We'd both realized we had gotten married too young and didn't have any experience with anyone much different from ourselves, had not seen what was on the other side of the mountains. We only went out with, well you know, just other young people. And when we got older we were curious, felt like we'd missed something fun, important."

Young women are curious about marriage and ask intimate questions about cheating, sex frequency, kinky sex, what it's like after a couple of years, what it's like to get divorced. They haven't met anyone who would talk frankly and openly about something they want to know. Preparation meets opportunity.

Discuss sex matter of factly. Your attitude is sex is wonderful and natural. She asks intimate questions only after she trusts you, along about the tenth conversation.

Plant this seed when the opening presents itself, you will reap an abundant harvest in the coming months, "I've learned the hard way, you don't have to marry everyone you date." It's usually when she mentions a girl friend who's having a hard time after breaking up with someone.

One more seed. Say in plain English, "It's important to just enjoy life and have fun when one is young. Responsibilities come soon enough." But not to her or about her. Express this when discussing a friend's son dropping out of college.

Drop subtle hints to get her thinking about the advantages of older men, not you in particular. Such as, what dicks young males are, how you used to f, f, and f 'em, too. Or, how important you used to think having a cool car was. Think about what a genuine jerk you were at Jimmy's age. That'll help with this part.

FOOT IN MOUTH STORIES

Ginny was a surprising first date. She wore me out. I was astounded with her ability and desire. We had a second date better than the first. A few days later we had lunch at her request.

Obliquely she wanted to know my views on marriage. Directly I said, "I'm never getting married again." I didn't get to date her again. Two months later she married a Vegas black jack dealer she had known for two weeks. She got divorced in six months.

I had gotten to know the 22 year old, beautiful Diane through one of my friends who worked at the same restaurant. When Diane finished early we would talk and play backgammon while I waited for my friend.

After several evenings of this across two weeks I asked her to lunch. She one upped me and suggested a movie. She had to work Saturday night and Sunday, so we left it at she'd call me Monday and we'd figure it out from there.

We kept playing and talking about men and life and relationships and marriage and water skiing and such. She looked at me and said suggestively, "I'm not going to bed with you when we go out." The right response was and is, "Okay." But no, I was working on a buzz, so I was witty and clever, "Yeah right.

Not until we're married," and laughed. So did she.

She didn't call. I went to the restaurant and asked if something had come up. She said, "You just want to screw me." I responded, after a few moments to recover from the shock, "I'd like to get to know you." She replied, "I won't waste my time with anyone who doesn't want to get married." A three-second remark destroyed a month's work. Drinking and driving is almost as dangerous and drinking and talking.

Maybe you'll learn something, a little, from my mistakes? If so, you won't talk your way out of a Diane before you've even had a chance. And you won't destroy the potentially grand affair with a Ginny. Can you learn from the mistakes of others? We'll see, after you learn how to *Date Her*.

"I don't care where we go,
I don't care what we do,
I don't care pretty baby,
just take me with you."

Prince

"Let's spend the night together."

Mick Jagger

Date Her

What is a date? The next-to-last step of courtship. It's any activity undertaken in the pretext of having fun, giving her time to decide, consciously or subconsciously, if she wants you to take the last step.

It took persistence, time and patience to interest her and prove yourself. Even now that she's attracted, more of the same is required to reach, then take the last step, and penetrate her.

WHERE SHE'S COMING FROM

The oldest guy she's dated was 28, Randy Red-Porsche, and you know how he treated her. She doesn't want that happening again.

She enjoys talking with you, flirting with you and sees little risk in being a casual friend of yours or for liking you as an interesting person. But you're not a boy. You've read this time and time again, she sees you as a powerful, dangerous male. Dating you is the big time. It's new, exciting, glamorous but, "Gee, pretty scary, too, I don' know."

On a date she knows there will be a new role for her, one radically different from the one she's been playing at your office or at her work across the past weeks or months. She has no experience to draw on and no confidence in her ability to handle you. She thinks you have a magic, slick way of getting her on her back before she even knows what happened.

She's not just worried about dealing with you, she's thinking about the consequences. "What will Debbie think if I, for real, go out with him. What if we're seen together? What if Jimmy finds out? What if? What if?"

She has to answer those questions herself. Don't acknowledge them. Anticipate her concerns. Suggest a date that'll dispense with most. You know her. What's she worried about? Use your big head.

She's struggling against everything parents, church, society, boyfriend and girl friends have drilled into that pretty young head and heart of hers. It's nearly impossible for her to make a date with you, the first time. It's like a Hell's Angel asking you to to come over to his place for some anal sex. It usually takes a pseudo date or two before she's ready for a real date.

ACCIDENTAL OR PSEUDO DATES

Ideally, the first date "just happens." When it "just happens," her resistance to going out with someone she can't marry is dissolved. She doesn't have to take responsibility, it "just happened."

Remember Freud's quote back in *Your Motives*? Things don't really "just happen," now do they. Make it "just happen" the first time. "Just happen" to need a ride home from work, the club meeting or class. "Just happen" to be at the same party. "Just happen" to know how to hook up her stereo or adjust her carb. If you have a string of pearls, Katy at the coffee shop, Denice at the print shop and Laurie at the office, the opportunity for it to "just happen" is tripled.

When it doesn't "just happen," the best first date is a pseudo date, one she views as completely innocent, something she'd do with a friend. To her, and anyone she's worried about, it sounds like and looks like she's only "going to do something," not go out. She can tell her peers about it without raising their eyebrows and her own suspicions. Even if she suspects, most do, she still needs to pretend it's not a date.

The purpose of a pseudo date is for her to be with

you in a new setting, enjoy herself and be attracted strongly enough to want a real date. The purpose of real dates is for her to enjoy herself and be attracted strongly enough to want you to take the last step of courtship.

DEFINING DATES

A "real date" is when you suggest a future get together: meeting her for a drink, lunch, brunch or dinner, a game of tennis, racket ball or a bicycle ride; teaching her how to do something, backgammon, tennis, scuba dive, ride a motorcycle, drive a stick shift, taking her anywhere, Disneyland, beach, mountains, desert, a friend's pool, the movies, a concert, a play, a Laker game, the Comedy Store, day skiing, dirt bike riding, even a ride to look at homes decorated for Christmas.

A real date isn't real if it just happens "spontaneously." For example, you "just happen" to be in the coffee shop about the time she's getting off. She mentions the home decorating contest up in the heights. You suggest going up to look the winners over, adding you have to back here in an hour. Then, you two go directly to her car (she feels safer, more in control) and leave.

"Kinda dates" are when she asks you for a real date. The best!

Learning how to do something from her is not a real date. She's just showing you how to dive, play tennis or anything else where the roles are reversed, young teaching old. But you have to meet her there, not take her. And, when asking her to teach you, it cannot sound, look, smell or feel like you're asking her out. It "just happened."

"Pseudo dates" are: fixing her car, hooking up her stereo, helping her move, editing her term paper, doing her income tax, working on a class or club project together, going out with a bunch of people for a few after class or to lunch from work, maybe having her help you pick out some new clothes at the mall. Make these "just happen," too.

PSEUDO DATES

The pseudo date appears to help her or be safe and fun. Command, don't ask. "Bring your car over to my house at 10 on Saturday. It sounds like something I can fix in 20 minutes." Or, "I'll hook it up for you, tonight about 7. Won't take long. What's your address?" Maybe this, "I'm going up to the college about 5 and shoot some baskets. Come on up. Let's see how good you really are."

When she asks you, don't be obviously delighted. Take your time. Pretend you're thinking about it, then time limit it. For example, she asks, "Could you take a look at my car? It's making a funny noise when I put it into park."

You're response, after mulling it over, considering if you can put Rachel Welch and Lauren Hutton on hold is, "Yeah, but I can't tell much unless I can jack it up and get under there. Bring it over when you get off. Here's my address. I live just up the street a few blocks. I've got to go out at 7, though." This is from my real world, Janet, 20. We lasted three months after two false starts. She was skittish, I was patient.

Some girls will shake those titties and ask you to work for them, then have nothing more to do with you. Who cares? You didn't have much else to do on a Saturday morning. Getting taken is the only way you learn to tell the users from the rest.

YOUR ATTITUDE WHEN SUGGESTING A PSEUDO DATE. Relaxed and casual, one friend to another. It's not important to you if it's yes or no. You're only commanding or suggesting "doing something," not asking her for a date, so who cares what she says. When steeled for rejection, you will be.

When She Doesn't Agree. If she's busy, "no biggie." Maybe next week. Don't say that, just radiate it.

She'll say "no" or "maybe" because it's too soon and scares her or she's not interested. Drop it. Talk about something else. By suggesting a pseudo date she knows you're interested. By not persisting, show her you're not that interested. If you apply pressure, she'll say "yes," then stand you up.

Trying to talk her into it doesn't work. It detracts from her image of you. Any man who's strong and powerful doesn't have to try. If you do, she finds you less attractive and it forces her to face facts: she wants to date you. That's an issue she's been avoiding, subconsciously waiting for it to "just happen." If you're patient it still might but if you push, you'll never get that first date with her, the one you've worked months for. Don't push.

But guess what? A few hours after declining she'll tell one of her friends you asked her out. You're on her mind. She'll wonder what it would have been like to go out with a man. Self doubt begins, can she "get you?" She's challenged.

Don't go back to her for a week. You've got her right where you want, thinking about you and hoping you'll try again. Don't. Just smile and be friendly, kinda happy to see her. She must believe she's not going to get another chance. You're just friends. Talk about skiing or where you've been on a trip. Ask her what she's been up to.

Now she really begins to wonder if she's "got it." Strange game? Yes. Necessary? Damn right. Be patient for two weeks. Wait for her to ask you but use your big head, give her an opening. If she doesn't ask, go to the next pearl. Don't come back to this one for a couple of weeks, then be friendly but standoffish. She has to ask you or practically beg you to ask her. If it's absolutely necessary, command, then be indifferent to her answer. If she makes excuses, congratulations, you've met your first young cock tease. There'll be more.

HER ATTITUDE ON A PSEUDO DATE. On some level she knows it didn't "just happen." She's nervous and on guard. This is much different from talking with you at the office, her work or after class.

In the back of her head she still thinks you may be the Hill Side Strangler even if she's gotten to know you pretty well over the past couple of months. She's also concerned you may be just another dirty old man trying to screw her.

She's new at this and feels pressure. She's never around anyone over 28 unless it's at work. She has no idea what to expect, has no idea how to behave or what to say. To her, there's something adults do that's different. The more attracted she is, the more excited, but the more worried about embarrassing herself.

HOW TO BEHAVE ON A PSEUDO DATE. Keep it all business. If she came over to have you look at her car, work on it. Offer her a beer if you're drinking one. Offer her another when you have another. Stay in the garage and don't try to move into the house. If she ends up hanging out with you after the car's done, fine.

You've got the chance, finally, to show her you're much more interesting, far more fun and attractive than any boy. Talk with her. Show yourself, your values and life view. Plant those seeds if the opportunity presents itself or if you can tactfully create the opening. Mention different things you like to do, unusual places to go, adult, fun activities. Something "safe" her boyfriend would never do. A matinee play, lunch at the Sheraton, skeet shooting. Jimmy takes her to 5-keg parties, Stallone-kills-everyone movies, or for a really big thrill, to the Grand Prix of Motocross at the coliseum. She wants to get dressed up and go out, like a woman.

Don't make any moves unless you're willing to bet your entire future with her on it, not to mention all the time and energy you've put into this so far. Even if she's radiating, "sweep me off my feet," nothing is lost by being patient. She wouldn't be here if you didn't have a chance. You've come this far after six weeks of talking with her. Don't ruin it now by being a pushover.

She's probably testing you to see if you really are a nice guy. In that case any pass is the same as slapping her face. If she's naive enough to think you're only working on her car, making even a little pass is the same as grabbing her tits.

The goal of pseudo dates is to let her see you're a

man, much better than boys, someone she could have fun with, someone she'd like to date. Don't forget it.

REAL DATES - DON'T ASK

To kill your chances, use these phrases: "Would you like to," "If you're not busy," "Can you." Suggest, don't ask permission. "I like talking with you. Let's have brunch Sunday, at Charlie Brown's." Make statements. Be positive. You're in charge here.

When she has other plans stay relaxed and confident. Remain cordial and friendly. There's tomorrow and a tomorrow after that. If you've built the foundation, the rest will follow. If you pressure her she'll agree then stand you up.

At the end of a sustained conversation it's too late to suggest a date. It must happen "naturally" during the conversation. If you wait until she's leaving, you look desperate, unattractive.

Do not, I say again, do not suggest a date on the first pseudo date. Let her go away and think to herself, "He's pretty cool, for being so old. I like him." After that soaks for a couple of days, talk with her under any pretext. Slow and easy. Ask how the car's doing or the stereo's working. See what the vibes are like before proceeding. A second pseudo date may be best.

Remember your unspoken attitude from seventy pages ago? *"Going out with me is natural. I'm attracted to you, you're attracted to me. You have a choice, a man or lots of boys."*

You're relaxed. You know she wants to go out with you, will go out with you, if you proposition her the right way. You'd like to date her but you're not dying to. It would be cool but if she says "no," it's not even a slight ripple in your world.

FIRST DATES. Use your big head. What has she mentioned across the past two months? Suggesting a drink is fine. It's not much to ask for, it's got a built-in time limit and it makes her feel grown up. But if you think she's still anxious, neutral turf makes it easier for her to accept. She knows bars and clubs are your territory.

Lunch at the park, like adults do it impresses her and she feels like a woman, not a girl. There, you're both equally distant from home base. No one is too defensive. But it's more of a commitment unless you add, "I've got to be back by 2." You only need an hour, the first time.

Sunday brunch at an expensive hotel is great, if during the suggestion it's clear you have to be somewhere at 3 pm. This puts on the time limit, making it easier to accept.

A dinner date is even a bit much for a woman to bite off. It implies dinner and. Save it for third or forth dates.

Your place is verboten. She has to be on guard. Suggesting her place makes her think you're married. She's not so dumb, she reads *Cosmopolitan*.

Her Attitude On The First Date. You're something brand new to her. She's been out with a boy or a young man hundreds of times but never a man. To her, it's like the first date with Jimmy when he took her to the prom in his dad's car. She didn't know what to do then, she's not sure what to do now. You're that different.

It's exciting and scary. She doesn't want to look like a foolish little girl in front of a man. She's afraid you'll laugh at her or pull some smooth maneuver and screw her. The younger she is, the more likely it is she will stand you up. She gets scared at the last minute and is too ashamed to call and tell the truth or to even lie. More later on handling this common occurrence.

She's not like her 27 year old counterparts. She doesn't want to hurry into the bedroom on the first date. She has to have, and needs all the preliminaries. She does not want to be a notch on another Red-Porsche's gun and she isn't interested in putting a 43 year old notch on her gun, like some 30 year olds.

Your Attitude On The First Date. First dates are tense times for everyone of any age. She's especially uptight being with someone old enough to be her father. Don't talk about the age difference unless she forces the issue directly. It does not exist.

It is as natural as sunrise to be out with you. There is nothing unusual about this date.

Don't plan and scheme. Let things happen naturally. Just enjoy her company. The more relaxed you are, the more she'll relax. Don't try to impress her. Be yourself. Expect nothing.

There have been several young women who have come over to my place "just for a drink" and pulverized my pelvis. That only happened after I stopped thinking and hoping it would. As I preach, it was her idea. I was surprised every time. Expect nothing.

Yeah, I know I told you not to suggest your place. That's during the first two years at this. After that you'll have enough confidence to pull it off. Want to see if I'm right? Go ahead punk, make my day, bet eight hard weeks of your life on a three-second ten-word "suggestion."

YOUR HEAD ON THE FIRST DATE AND ALL OTHERS. A high sperm count dramatically interferes with everything you try to do. If necessary, take matters into your own hand before the first date. Loneliness, boredom or lack of sobriety also prevent you from doing the right things at the right moments. I guarantee too much booze prevents correct decisions at each turning point. Control thyself.

More than three drinks and I'm too aggressive, unable to read her correctly. Absolutely straight, I usually don't have enough steel in my balls to even suggest the first date. Building my "confidence" with Shelly helped me begin to know myself, and how! Know thyself.

HOW TO BEHAVE ON THE FIRST DATE. Be prompt about picking her up or meeting her. Have her home when you said you would. Don't get swept up in the whole thing. Demonstrate you're a gentleman. Keep your wits about you. Don't drink too much and get loose.

Tactfully control her intake. She's scared, using Dutch courage, too. If she gets plowed that will be the end. The next day she'll remember, "My gawd. I puked in his new Jag." She'll judge herself the complete asshole. Her biggest fear came true. In front of a man, she behaved like a naive little girl. She'll never even want to look at you again. This happened to me twice, not in a new Jag (damn!) but it ruined everything all the same.

No No's. Don't talk about sex, your children, ex-wife, what a shit your boss is. Don't be impatient with other drivers, slow waiters or be cynical about life. No nostalgia trips about the 60's or 50's. No flowers or gifts. No blatant flirting with her. No, absolutely no looking at other females. No questions regarding boyfriend status.

No matter what happens, don't be a pushover. This is a recording. You're only moderately interested.

Yes Yes's. Touch her at every socially acceptable opportunity from the first to last moment, helping with her sweater, admiring her ring or finger nails, bracelet, necklace (careful Buddy!) Patting her on the back for a great joke or other excuse. Otherwise, no touching, period. She can touch you.

Open doors, light cigarettes, order for her, walk on the outside and other gentlemanly behavior. She'll love it. Otherwise, only moderate attentiveness. Keep this affair out of the shitter! No accommodating. You make the decisions without consulting her. Be a man. Be in charge.

Champagne is fun and exotic. He drinks beer. Opening a second bottle is obvious. Don't cause her to think, "He's trying to get me drunk so he can take advantage of me. Mother told me about guys like this." There are big, not blatantly big, bottles of champagne, 1.5 liters. Buy one for the first-date picnic, beach trip or whatever you concoct.

Talking. Keep the conversation light and pleasant. Avoid controversial subjects. Reveal your likes and dislikes in movies, television, sports, food, travel, drinks, games, and such. Ask her about similar subjects. Arranging a second date is much easier if you find out where you two fit together other than anatomically.

Work into the conversation things you like to do and places you like to go. When she reciprocates, ask some questions, then add, "That sounds like it might be fun. Let's go there sometime," and see what her reaction is. Don't firm it up even when she's very positive. Wait.

If she knows how to do something you don't, see if she'd like to teach you, "sometime." If she knows of an interesting restaurant, again say, "it might be fun" to go there "sometime."

Setting Up A Second Date. If she asks you, with a time and day, fine, she's mature and serious. Go ahead and make a date. But when she asks in general, say, "That sounds like fun. Let me check my schedule. I'll call you."

Don't appear to have an open calendar or to be willing to shift things around to fit her offer. You're a man, a busy grown-up doing grown-up things. You're powerful. You don't accommodate (sounds like?) your life to a young woman's schedule. You're the catch here. Got it?

I ended up with matters in my own hand every time I've said, "When can we get together again?" or, "When will I see you again?" and even, "Let's do this again, soon." Let her know in plain English you had fun and enjoyed being with her. Don't suggest a second date.

A SECOND DATE, MAYBE

Even if something's been semi-setup, wait a few days, then call and talk for a while. See how the vibrations are. If they're positive or neutral, suggest, don't ask, a non-romantic date. If she's negative, shine it and wait for her to call you and ask for a date. It'll be a long wait, like the rest of your life.

After the first date, it's the same as with a woman. If she doesn't want to go out with you again, she won't. Either you scared her or she thinks you're a dick. There is this difference, a young woman has to deal with her guilt for going out with you, someone old enough to be her father and for cheating on Jimmy. There's not much you can say or do, she feels guilty, period.

For her to want a second date with you, the first date has to be a great experience. Have fun together. You want her to think, "Gee, I went out with a man! It was fun, not perverted. He's goes to cool places. Wonder why he didn't even try to kiss me good night? Maybe he doesn't like me."

WHAT GOES WRONG BEFORE THE FIRST DATE

Julie has a sometimes boyfriend but she wants to go out with me. The other girls who work with her and who know me encourage her to "go for it." We were going to get together tonight and do some slammers. She said she'd call after taking her mother to the airport. She didn't. Two years back I would have been on the phone a half an hour ago. Now, I'm going finish this paragraph, have a beer and watch "Sports Center." No matter what the song says, you still have time for the waiting game, even in September.

I should have known. She couldn't have, with pre-meditation, come over here after taking her mother to the airport. She wouldn't have to go home. Even if she did want to wear me out on the first date, she wants it to "just happen." Planning it and scheduling it makes it too real. See what I mean about not suggesting your place? I should know better! I wrote the book.

I'll move on down my string of pearls and wait for my subconscious to figure out a way to make my first date with Julie "just happen."

There's such a thing as waiting too long. Young women have short attention spans. Three days to an 18 year old seems like three weeks to us. Young males are always trying. After ten days you're history. You were only another pearl on her string, too.

If she said she'd call and didn't, wait a couple of days. Call her. Be pleasant and casual. Wait for an explanation. If one is not forthcoming, move on to the next pearl. Nothing I've done is effective when she doesn't hold up her end of an agreement.

She's too afraid to date you. There's nothing you can do to change her mind. Learn from your mistakes.

Review everything that went on. Usually I came on too fast or too hard and she only agreed to call because it was easier than saying she didn't want to date me.

You were an interesting but dangerous distraction. It was fun and exciting to talk with you and to daydream about riding you, but when it came down to actually picking up the phone she got frightened and felt perverted for being interested in you.

I've found, "Well, call me when you're not so scared," is no more effective than being pushy. She thinks I said, "I'm willing to wait for you because I don't have any balls."

It's necessary to fold 'em, step back and focus your efforts elsewhere. Don't waste any more time on her being patient and persistent. After a couple of more months of boys and young men she may be ready to take the plunge, maybe not.

HELPFUL DATING HINTS FROM HELOISE-DON

Let her drive your car if she doesn't scare you to death. She loves to drive and it makes her feel grown-up. Have her sign your credit card voucher for the same reasons. Let her make room reservations using your credit card number.

She tells her roommate you're "just a friend" not a lover. Carla told Connie that and Jean told Mona the same thing. Cooperate, she is afraid her peers will think she's loose, crazy or both. It is necessary to charm the roommate (Teddy) when the time comes and win her approval.

Don't spend money beyond your means on dates one through three, then try to save on the forth date. She'll get withdrawal pains. Doing something unusual she can tell her friends about is better.

SECOND DATES

The horse races. A play. Something big, something different, something men do. Nothing romantic. Not dinner at an elegant restaurant. Nothing at your place.

I am not willing to go to a rock concert, period, even with a 9.8. I do not like the scene or the people attending and I feel out of place as well as "out of it to the max." I can tolerate club sized performances of rockers I like.

You cannot get tired on her. Take a nap so you can be alive and energetic. You must keep up with her. If you're in aerobic shape, and you'd better be, you will have plenty of endurance.

Everything is done about the same as the first date. Expressing more likes and dislikes, encouraging her to do the same. Look for matches and fits.

Depending on everything, yes, everything, your instincts in particular, you can, possibly, perhaps, maybe, suggest a third date, during the second but not at the end of it. Calling her a few days later is still the best course to follow when in doubt. This is a recording. You're only moderately interested.

There should be more touching, some of it not socially appropriate but not too romantic. Depending on everything, yes, everything, a gentle, not lustful, good night kiss is possible. Listen to your instincts. Tina fucked me four times on the second date. That's right, she, fucked me, the wonderfully insatiable 19 year old thing. We're in the eighth month of our affair as I'm writing this.

THIRD DATES AND BEYOND

Prepare to take the last step. She's no different from a woman. Now is the time for romantic dates, movies, dinners, walks on the beach, kissing and hugging, some fondling. It's only a matter of time when you've gotten this far.

"Use the Force, Luke, use the Force." Pay attention to your feelings. It may be appropriate to suggest pop corn in front of the fire place or champagne and hors d'oeuvres at your house. I don't need a transition paragraph here, do I? You can't wait to turn this page!

> *"Into your bedroom she brings:*
> *little knowledge, some experience*
> *and great expectations."*
>
> **The Author**

> *"In the game of love*
> *it's not important*
> *if you win or lose*
> *but whether or not you score."*
>
> **Woody Allen**

Sex With Her

Her motivation's not a bit different from a woman's, she wants a cock inside her, thrusting. But, she wants it like it's been in her secret daydreams and fantasies across the past five years.

AN ANALOGY FOR UNDERSTANDING

She has a new body, relatively. It's only four or five years old. It's a hell of a lot different from the one she had for 15 years. This model's got big, round curves and sometimes seems to have a mind of it's own. She's gradually gotten used to it, kinda. "But it's, you know, like, well, like, I don't know, empty, uh, like, not full." *Translation:* She always wants more.

She's owns a powerful new motorcycle but has no idea what it's got or how fast it'll go. Jimmy rides it but never gives it much of a workout. He doesn't get very far. After getting it all revved up, he pops his clutch. It feels good but frustrating. She wants it taken to the limit, red lined in fifth gear. She's dying to know, "What'll it really do?" Trouble is, she wants to fly but she's terrified of crashing and burning.

SEDUCTION FOLLOWS UNDERSTANDING

She does not want to feel out of control. She's excited and scared at the same time. Don't overwhelm her. Make her feel good but don't give her the "full on" demonstration of what it's like to get seriously fucked even if that was, and is, one of her main reasons for dating you.

She can't appreciate the full spectrum of your knowledge, ability and experience until she gets used to the idea of being in bed with you. The fourth or fifth time you can give her what she's been waiting for. That doesn't mean the fifth time the first night either, you satyr, you.

She doesn't want you to think she's inexperienced, embarrassed, ignorant, naive or innocent. Be strong but gentle and sensitive. Don't let your little head do the thinking.

Concentrate on her. Pay attention to what gives her pleasure. Don't expect her to tell you, read her mind and her body. Use your experience and knowledge. Ensure she has a wonderful, pleasure filled time the first few engagements.

Boys come first, literally. Young men are not able to sustain intercourse. This alone gives you the edge to become her lover. Don't blow your edge. That's her job but not for weeks. That's all Jimmy ever wants. You're different. You love to go down on her and don't expect her to reciprocate.

SEDUCING HER

This date with her, the third, forth or tenth, is natural and normal. Act that way. You are not going to try anything. It will be her idea at her speed. She'll go to bed with you. It may not be tonight but she will. It is not now or never.

And, you certainly didn't invite her over saying anything like, "Don't worry, I won't make a pass at you." Let fantasy reign.

When she was here the last time and glanced in your bedroom, it didn't look like a pleasure palace, did it? Tell me there aren't any mirrors on the ceiling or even on the walls! It does look masculine and it better be neat and clean like the rest of your place.

There are no female products or leftovers anywhere. The whole house looks like only a single adult male lives here. You don't have pictures of your children displayed. You don't even have any pictures of your ex.

The living room is not set up for seduction, the lights down low, fireplace glowing and romantic music on softly. The champagne is in the refrigerator where it always is, not waiting in an ice bucket. Impressionable, gullible young men who read *Playboy* do shit like that.

She expects you to be confident, powerful and in charge. Be that. Don't act like a boy, in a hurry to ram it home. You're not like Jimmy. Take your time. She's different, special to you. You're special to her because you're different.

A boy hurries down the field, using plays she's seen a hundred times before. He never does anything unexpected. By the time he's "inside the ten," she's barely warmed up, but he's wound up, only focused on scoring. She puts in the short yardage defense team (strong, pushy resistance). He forces. She tightens the defense. He fumbles. She recovers, the ball as well as her composure, and becomes defense oriented.

Control your drinking. Keep your wits about you and your focus on her body language and overall mood. Understand her resistance when it comes, as it will. It means you're moving down field too fast or she's testing your power. You're response every time is unspoken, radiated, "Okay. If we don't tonight, no biggie. We will."

When the kissing and fondling start, no matter how receptive she is, don't pour on full voltage, you'll short circuit her. If she feels out of control her only solution is to panic stop. Build the excitement, then back off and let her keep control. After you start again she'll be willing, and able, to go farther without slamming on the brakes. The whole evening has this pattern.

Your game plan is different. You keep her off balance during the preliminaries by doing the unexpected, especially as the foreplay is nearing completion. By being unpredictable you prevent her from making a goal line stand. That's what she does to a boy. Don't be a boy.

Her Thoughts. *Mmmm. Nice soft lips. Yuck, what if he has false teeth? Oh, I guess he doesn't. Mmm. He smells good. My, what a romantic he is. Mmmm. Should I play hard to get? Ummm. . . Why'd he stop?*

Go to the bathroom and listen to me one more time. Don't let her get to the point where she has to dig in her heels and use her will power to prevent "going all the way." Build and stop. Begin again but go farther, then stop again until you're on the one yard line. That's the last time I'm going to tell you.

Now go back out there and talk for awhile. Then start again.

Her Thoughts. *Nice strong hug. Umm. Oh, he's going for my tit. I should push his hand away a couple of times? Umm, feels good. Ummmm. Why am I getting so wet?*

She loves her tits squeezed. You're kissing and hugging passionately. Slide your hand up there. Don't stay long. Be different.

Her Thoughts. *I shouldn't let him touch me there. Ohh . . . I'm drinking too much? Oh! . . . Ummmm. He stopped?*

You shift a bit as you slow down. She "accidentally" brushes against your cock.

Her Thoughts. *Jeez, pretty big, but not as big as Randy's was.*

Get up and make another drink. Then take the phone off the hook. While you're doing that:

Her Thoughts. *Maybe I shouldn't tonight. Next week Jimmy'll be at the races. I wonder why he stopped?*

Bring the drinks and sit down. Talk for awhile. Then begin again. Take your time but go farther.

Her Thoughts. *He's so gentle. Oooh, he knows where it is. Ummmm. What if I smell funny? Oooh, oh, he's putting my hand on his thing. Mmmm. He's really hard!*

It's forth down, six inches, pardon the pun, to score. After a two month, sustained drive what play should you call? "Full back over right guard, take her right here on the couch?" Nope. Too predictable. She's used to power plays like that, from boys. Keep your pants on!

Come on! You're Kenny "The Snake" Stabler's age. You got here by being different from the competition, you're going to score by staying different. **Time out!**

Go put on another tape. Huddle with yourself. Think about it. While you're doing that her curiosity is yelling, *"Let's see what it's really like."* Her conscience is yelling, *"You slut! You're cheating on Jimmy."* But then, her throbbing pussy pleads, *"Go for it! Lock onto that cock."*

To you it was no big deal. You interrupted the session just when she was getting into it. You're different.

Don't power it in, do the unexpected. Call the quarter back option. As the play develops you can run it in yourself, pitch out to the sweeping back, or, if it's all blocked up, pass, back across the grain to the "tight end," *she'll* be "wide open."

"Triple option right. On Two!" **Time in!** Let the kissing and fondling go on and on until she's white hot. "Hut one."

Her Thoughts. *This is too much. Come on!*

"Hut Two!" Don't ask, just do it. Take her by the hand and confidently lead her to the bedroom.

She wants you make love to her, not screw her. Do that, beginning with the way you undress her. Now that you're in bed, don't ask, just do whatever you want, gently but firmly.

Her Thoughts. *My, OH Myyy. I never knew a tongue could feel . . . Ohh my . . . UMMuh . . . yes, YES!*

She's accustomed to a minute, maybe two, after he rams it in, then he comes and rolls off. Enter gently. Sustain your rhythmic thrusting.

Her Thoughts. *Umm . . . Umm . . . Oh my . . . Umm . . . nice. Ummmm . . . He's good . . . Ohh . . . Am I doing it right? He's . . . breathing . . . Uh Uhhh . . . so hard. Uhhh . . . What if he has a heart attack . . . Ohhhh . . . here it comes . . . Uh Uhhh Yessss. UMMUHH . . . UHH . . . OHHH . . . More. More . . . MORE!*

She'll have a burst of guilt, feel like a slut. Acknowledge her feelings, don't lecture or give advice. Hold her gently, sensitively. Later, compliment her on making you feel good. For Christ's sake, don't ask her if she came.

Things will be different now. *Phase Two* has begun.

Phase Two

The Courtship: find, meet, talk with and date made up Phase One. It lasted one day or three months. *The Affair:* date, talk with, make love and deal with each other makes up Phase Two. It can last two nights or two years.

It's a new, forbidden impossible situation, filled with pleasure, fraught with danger. The everyday relationship isn't much trouble. The routine stuff's about the same as with a 28 year old except for the problems associated with your young lover's immaturity but that's not the big difference.

The big, and I mean major difference is the far, far greater intensity of emotions you both experience. The highs feel twice as good, the lows feel bottomless. However, you two must make passionate love for weeks before these feelings begin to cause problems.

HER REASONS TO KEEP DATING YOU

In Phase Two with Jimmy she must always behave like a future wife. She has to manipulate continually to maintain control of the relationship. With you, Phase Two's different. She knows there will be no wedding bells. She can just relax and enjoy.

She appreciates you, looks forward to her time with you. You behave like a gentleman, always treating her with respect. Experience across the years enables you to understand her moods and not take it personally when she's a bitch. You listen sensitively, without interrupting, to her problems. And, when her anguish comes, you comfort and console her, accepting it without telling her to stop acting like a baby, as Jimmy does. When she makes a young person's mistake you don't give her hell for not knowing what she should have done, like Jimmy does. You know what makes the world work, easily fixing life problems Jimmy has no idea how to even begin solving. Always thoughtful and considerate of her needs, you take your time in bed. You don't want blow jobs all the time, Jimmy does.

You're as special to her as she is to you, as different to her as she is to you, as exciting to her as she is to you. But things get complicated in Phase Two when powerful, pleasant emotions arise.

AFTER GRAND TIMES, PROBLEMS BEGIN

You two have just returned from your first romantic weekend together in Lake Tahoe. Every night was filled with caring, sensual, satisfying sex. The days were each an exciting adventure of new, fun, adult activities. Don't let her have more than 24 hours away from you.

After this intimate, delightful time together she innocently wants to share her joy. She tells her friends how happy and exciting her life is.

ENVY CAUSES SECOND THOUGHTS. At least one "friend" will feign pleasure at the news, then, within a minute, sneak in a comment designed to devastate her. It will be innocent sounding advice or innocent sounding concern or innocent sounding question: "You wouldn't want to marry someone that old, would you?" It makes no difference what the "friend" says, his or her purpose is to make your lover feel cheap, foolish and immoral.

Another "friend," in the guise of saving her, will lecture on the immorality and impracticality of continuing with you, "I know this really is none of my business BUT, I don't want you to get hurt. You'd better be careful. Those older guys are, well, uh, uh, he might be using you."

Her "friends" have no understanding or empathy. They are not pleased for her and see her happiness as threatening. Perhaps it puts them in touch with how boring and empty their own lives are, dating the same boyfriend for two years, grinding away at a menial job or endlessly trying to finish college. Secretly they too, want to have a fling but don't have the courage of your young lover, so they try to destroy her.

Your young woman is not together enough to realize why her "friends" would do this except to "help" her. She's not yet seen how small and vicious people are, stomping on someone else's happiness because they, themselves, are unhappy.

Don't wait until after she hears this destructive crap to explain the motivation and results of envy. She wants to be a good person but isn't far enough down the adult trail to know, really know, deep inside she has to live by her own rules, not those drummed into her by our culture, then invoked by "friends" when it serves their petty ends. When the opening presents itself in Tahoe gently mention to her what may happen with her friends when she gets back. Prevention is the only cure for the disease of envy.

HER OWN SECOND THOUGHTS. Even without "friends" like this, being alone gives her too much time to think. It's been so good she begins considering the long run possibilities of the relationship. Suddenly she remembers you two won't be getting married and living happily ever after! In a state of shock she critically reviews exactly what her own rules and regulations permit. She starts to feel like a bad girl. The excitement, the pleasure of being appreciated and feeling special vanish as her adrenaline flows. She can't remember what her reasons for being with you are, or rather, were.

Every relationship has to "lead somewhere." The longer she has, the more "reasons" she generates for never seeing you again. Soon she sees, ethically, the only thing to do is break it off. Once this happens her brakes get locked. She's in a four wheel skid. When you try talking with her she'll be steeled, invincible in her armor of rationalizations. It goes like this: it's not fair to you, it just couldn't work out, she's so sorry, didn't mean to hurt you, ad nauseam.

Think, think of a way of not letting her have more than a day to herself for a full week after the two of you return from the first grand weekend. Set it up beforehand, if possible. You want her to have solid proof it's not only okay, it's wonderful having an affair with you. The only hard evidence she can grasp is how happy she is and how good she feels. Only this can prevent friends "helping" her. This alone makes it possible for her to dismiss self doubts.

SHE COMES THEN GOES

Julie didn't want to get up and go home. She wanted to spend the night like "real lovers." "But," I objected, "you said you had to go because Jimmy was going to call at 11 and maybe come over. You can stay all night any time. Let's not take chances."

She developed a plan whereby she would spend the night when Jimmy was going to the desert with his buddies. She'd tell him she was going out "with the girls." When he called at 2 am, like he probably would, and get no answer, her story would be she got blitzed and spent the night at Debbie's. Complicated? Yes. Necessary? Uh huh. Did it ever happen? Nope.

By the time Friday got there she changed her mind. Spending the night was somehow bad. But going to bed with me in the afternoon when he was at work wasn't good, it just wasn't bad. A few weeks later she felt like even having lunch with me was bad and stopped seeing me altogether, for five whole days.

Her guilt trips ebb and flow. You have no more control over this than you do over the ocean's tides.

Don't let it freak you out. Hang in. Be patient. Listen and be empathetic but don't give advice or try to manipulate her into spending time with you. She has enough trouble dealing with all her other feelings. Just tell her you want to see her and drop it. She has to proceed or withdraw by her own values, based on her own needs and goals.

WHEN GOOD GETS BETTER - WE ALL WANT BEST

It makes no difference if she has a Leftover, a String Along or no boyfriend, she's having quite an experience. She doesn't understand why or how she can feel so good and have so much fun with you when it has no chance of leading anywhere. After six weeks she stops questioning and just accepts it.

But the better it is for the both of you the sooner she begins wondering what would happen if she broke it off with Jimmy. She forgets what you told her about the impossibilities. She wonders if the two of you can make it work. She wants it to lead somewhere not just continue as it is.

Every human being wants something good to get better. She's no different. But, she must regain her perspective or madness begins for you both. Ethically, you must put your foot down, gently at first and not let things get out of hand. This will be hard, as she will try to manipulate you, subtly at first. When you stand firm she'll threaten to end it and make other power moves. You have to stop with her at this point, for a few weeks or forever.

Don't get cocky! You're vulnerable to the same feelings and desires. There are hidden motives, secret longings and unmet needs lurking in your soul, too. More on that in a few pages.

POSITIVE LEADS TO NEGATIVE. As time passes, the wonderful, positive emotions you both experience and enjoy so much cause negative feelings to arise. Some of her unpleasant ones are: (1) Insecurity and fear you'll reject her for an older female. (2) Fear you're too powerful to control. (3) Guilt for enjoying sex with you when it isn't going anywhere. (4) Rejection when she can't participate in normal activities like going to your company's picnic. (5) Guilt for dating you and her boyfriend. (6) Fear her boyfriend, parents, friends or peers will find out. (7) Confusion and anger over your erratic behavior caused by your feelings. (8) Fear she will fall deeply in love with you when she knows it can't work.

You have powerful, disorienting emotions, too: (1) Insecurity and fear she'll drop you for another man. (2) Anger and confusion over how to relate to her when she's acting erratic because of her feelings. (3) Guilt, confusion and shame for not living up to your own standards of propriety, love, sex, honor, courage, et al. (4) Fear your company or others who can harm you will find out. (5) Rejection when you can't accompany her to normal events like a sorority dance. (6) Fear of falling deeply in love with her when you know it can't work.

Honesty Is Always The Best Policy. There's not much you can do about these emotions except understand you're not crazy when she begins exhibiting erratic behavior or you do, and worse, when you both do. You can resolve some of the problems caused by your feelings by sharing them with her.

Adult women expect and want you to be strong and rational at all times. Nearly all young women like it and can handle it when you're not. After you act like an asshole, and you will, apologize but try to explain where it came from, what you were feeling and thinking to make you behave so badly.

She's going through similar things. She'll understand and accept. You must do the same when she screws up. Let time pass. Cool down, both of you. Have courage and good will. Beyond this, you and she can only decide how much craziness you can live with, then call it quits when the limit is exceeded.

Sometimes she can see it was fear, frustration, confusion, doubt or whatever behind her bizarre behavior. It doesn't do much good to tell her that's the cause. Nobody accepts psychological analysis even from a shrink.

In short, there are problems caused by the strong emotions of Phase Two different from those with a woman. You will be the source of some, she will be the cause of others and our culture's rules will be create still more. Resolution depends on the honesty, courage, dedication and strength of you and your young lover. That's no different from any human relationship. The relationship with her is just far, far more emotionally intense. I love it, even after blowing . . . well you'll see in a few pages.

There are problems not caused by emotions, they arise when it's not clear *Who's In Charge Here?*

Who's In Charge Here?

In the early days I foolishly believed I didn't have to be on top, to be on top. I was so naive. Not knowing it was necessary to be in charge of everything I figured I could compromise on everything except major issues. After a few trashed me I asked for feedback. They told me in plain English, "I only like it when the man's in charge. You're too nice."

Back in the 70's there was a myth that men and women could have a relationship of equals. Well it was just that, a myth. There is no such thing and cannot be. One person is always in control. The relationship can be a three-minute conversation in a pickup bar, a six month affair or a ten year marriage. The person in charge is the one who won't take shit, the person most willing to say, and then do it, "No more. I quit."

MANIPULATION IS HER WAY OF LIFE

Remember mini-marriages? Does this sound familiar, ". . . *where they learn, practice and perfect the control and manipulation techniques they will use in their real marriages.*"

She sees nothing immoral about manipulating you. To her, all males must be manipulated. That's the way Mommy controls Daddy. It's how her friend's Mommies control their husbands, how sit-com Mommies control sit-com Daddies, and it's how soap opera females control soap opera males.

She's not a malicious, unethical person, it's just all she knows. Straightforward is not in her repertoire. She thinks it has to be this way. It's normal, everyone relates to each other like this. Even relationships with her girl friends are full of guilt inducing, finagling. Nobody's direct with anybody in her world.

WHAT SHE BELIEVES AND REALLY WANTS

She wants the man to be in charge and considers it proper and morally right even if she fights against it and tests you weekly. She doesn't like, admire or respect anyone she can control. She doesn't want another boy, she wants a man. Not a macho man who demands full time submission. But, you'd better believe she wants you to make her submit, from time to time, sexually and every other way.

A stronger one will constantly challenge you even over extremely small issues to see if you're still in charge. If you aren't, she's angry and let down. She didn't really want to be the boss.

Strong or not she tests you by standing you up, then calling with (1) "Sorry 'bout yesterday. Jimmy came by, couldn't call. Don't be mad. He's going to the desert tomorrow. Can I spend the night?" (2) She won't call until the next day and pretend she didn't test you. She says excitedly, "I can spend the night. Jimmy's going to the desert." (3) She'll go to the beach instead of coming over in the afternoon as agreed, then cops a plea, "Sorry, Pam, my best friend from school came by. I couldn't tell her 'bout you. Don't be mad. Can I spend the night tomorrow? Jimmy's going to the desert."

This is the only response that works, "I'm pissed off. We had a date. You didn't call. (Pause for effect.) No you can't spend the night. I have plans. Maybe some other time. Goodbye." CLICK!

She must believe the possibilities include you will never see her again. It takes an iron will to turn down a night with her early on, but turn it down you must if you hope to continue in a pleasurable way. If you take her shit now it only gets worse.

Being led around by the dick is only fun in the early training sessions, you know, when she rewards you for taking crap by rubbing your cock with her tonsils. If you trade blow jobs for her irresponsible behavior you lose her respect, becoming just another pussy whipped boy. Every time she gets "a better offer" she'll take it, knowing that soon you'll be a completely house broken puppy.

Some of you may think you can regain control later, believing you can maneuver and manipulate you way back to the helm after she finds out how great you really are. Lombardi and I wish you luck.

ACT LIKE A MAN

If you won't be manipulated or lied to you will retain control of the relationship. Stand firm and refuse to be treated badly. Behave like a man with plenty of self respect and you'll do fine.

Don't retaliate. Let her know in clear, easy to understand terms what is unacceptable behavior. Do not bluff. She will call it, I guarantee. When you get called you two will be finished or you're in for a long run of her shitty behavior.

I am absolutely committed to not putting up with anything, especially early on. I learned the hard way it's tough enough training her in the first place. It's impossible to re-train her. Be smarter than the dog, stay fully in charge for months.

BENEVOLENT DICTATORS

She knows you two are not equal. She knows you are the more powerful, knowledgeable person. In her view you are the male, therefore you are the leader. Get it through your head, she only knows one way of relating. You must live up to, and act out her idea of what a man is.

It's a shame but even letting her decide where to go for dinner is a sign of weakness to her. She thinks, "The man should decide these things." She has such limited experience she reads diplomatic as weak, considerate as accommodating (sounds like?) forgiveness as no balls.

If you're not willing to be in charge you will be out of control. Later on, like four months from now, after she realizes she can't take over, you can back off a little, not much.

Too bad control is an issue in older man-younger woman relationships but it is and after the first few dates it's "the" issue. I reluctantly accepted it. Accept it. But be a benevolent dictator.

STANDBY FOR SELF DESTRUCT

Most young women can have fun and enjoy being with you in and out of bed only if "We're not getting serious." She prefers lust to love in your eyes. Her boyfriend adores her or ignores her but he never lusts for her.

If she starts to fall in love it's okay in her mind only if you don't reciprocate. In this state the affair can continue for a while longer. Should you lose control and say or even behave in ways that mean "I love you" the end is at hand.

She can't handle it. My guess? It puts her in touch with what she's really doing, falling for someone she cannot marry. When you come back with similar feelings, expressed in words or otherwise, she has to face it. Confronted with *The Fact:* You're not marriable, her conclusion, "Let's end this right here, right now. It can't go anywhere."

The worst part is she ends up running the show when she thinks, feels or believes you care for her more than she cares for you. Even if you are insanely in love with her don't express it in deeds or verbally. If you do you'll also lose control of the relationship. What do I mean by "also?" Simple, you've already lost control of your feelings falling in love with someone half your age.

> *"Love, love, love*
> *Love is all you need*
> *All you need, all you need*
> *Love is all you need."*

For John, Paul, George and Ringo maybe. But you and Debbie?

Phase Two has one more big problem, the biggest. Well, let's see what happens when, not if, *Love Rears Its Beautifully Insane Head.*

Love Rears Its Beautifully Insane Head

It's near the end of the second month. Tension, more tension. She clenches, moans, then arches in orgasmic ecstasy and release. You thrust harder, abandoning all semblance of self. The flurry brings your sweet, oh so sweet, absolute surrender. You feel the pulse shoot into to her and see her smile. The second pulse sprays forth, she fades from sight. Your head jerks back. Whiteness envelops. Blackness descends. Ego gone, id rampages, pumping and spewing life into an empty universe.

As darkness lifts you collapse onto her. She embraces with youthful strength, holds you tight. Empty, fully empty, yet complete, lying there, face in the pillow, dimly aware of sweat everywhere she blends with you, slightly conscious of her nearly sated vagina caressing your softening cock. Slowly, you notice it's in rhythm with loving, warm hugs she never quite releases completely. Tighter, then tight. You lift your head in an attempt to turn toward her. She refuses, pressing her cheek firmly to yours. You yield, and wrap your arms around, joining her in an embrace of vulnerable oneness.

An eternity passes before she breaks the silence. She releases her grip slightly. With mouth beside your ear she softly utters the forbidden, "I love you so."

The long ago, self-inflicted deadness in your heart slithers away. You melt.

She strokes your head lovingly. Sadness wells, you tense, try to deny, try to resist, too late. A few hot teardrops fight past clenched eyelids, trickle down, onto her cheek. She knows! You try to escape. She merely crushes you to her with powerful, gentle acceptance, with innate motherly-womanly understanding far, far beyond her years. You yield, surrendering to the years, the empty, meaningless, lonely years of pain denied. You cry, deep from the soul, deep from the heart, anguished sobs of hurt, of rejection, of helplessness. She only holds you tighter, more tenderly, more understandingly.

When it's over, ashamed you try to rush away, somewhere, anywhere. She won't let you, makes you lie there and look at her. With words unspoken you see she admires you, respects you, not in spite of your tears and pain but because you are a man, a hu-man being. You two sit up on the edge of the bed. She takes your hand and looks into your face. She smiles, you smile, tears come into both your eyes. You start to explain, she shushes you.

She goes to the bathroom, you go to the kitchen and blow your nose, wash your face in the sink. As you're drying she glides into the room, unashamedly nude, throws her arms around your neck and smiles, you smile, she grins, you grin, she laughs, you laugh.

"Hey old man, can you get this up again?" she says, grabbing and flopping your flaccid member around. It stiffens slightly. She laughs with mock astonishment, "Not bad." She strokes it, you harden a bit more. She bends over and takes you into her mouth, all of you. Ramrod! She fakes gagging, giggles and leads you by the protuberance to the bedroom, throws you playfully on to the bed and climbs aboard.

You wear each other out during the next half hour. No tears this time, only exhaustion. You lie there holding each other and drift off to sleep, the sleep of contented animals, Bengal tiger and his young tigress.

By the middle of the third month these powerful, intense emotions have done their work. You've forgotten the impossibilities too, and given yourself free rein. You've said the forbidden words, from the heart many, many times and you're enthralled by the pure joy of loving again, giving again, living again.

Every day life-regenerating feelings sweep over you, through you, into you. You're excited, living energy courses through your veins. Born again! Happy for the first time in, what's it been now . . . My God! fifteen years. Fifteen years since you last felt like this, fifteen years since you knew what it meant to be alive, fully alive. Your perspective changes. Everything else becomes unimportant. Your thinking is clouded. You lose sight of reality and wish, then try to make this last forever.

FREE ADVICE

Just because it can't last forever is no reason to not love her and be loved in return. Shit, it didn't stop you the first time you fell in love, with your wife, did it? Don't let it stop you this time, either. So it doesn't last. What does?

My advice is simply to keep your perspective, the perspective 40 years on this planet has given you. Use what you know.

You know it can't last. But, if you don't know by now, *"Love is the grandest emotion, worth living for and sometimes worth dying for,"* you haven't learned diddly squat in four decades.

The high of love has a low. When it comes, as it will, don't whine and behave like a 27 year old. You knew, and know there is a price for everything. I say love is worth any price.

Decide if you're willing to pay the piper before you take the brakes off and go barreling into the abyss. She does not know it cannot last, she's a young woman. She honestly believes she can love you forever when she says she can. She sincerely feels deep, abiding love for you when she says she does.

When *The End* comes, accept it, then thank the gods for having had the chance to love again, to live again.

"You can't step in the same river twice. Only change is constant."

Heraclitus

"Thanks for the memories."

Bob Hope

The End

You've read about some of my affairs. All good things must come to an end. The longest was two and a half years, the shortest eleven days. The second longest was two years, the third longest, eight months. The rest, three months on average.

Of course there were untold numbers of young women I scared away, offended or who just plain didn't like me after one pseudo date. I wasted plenty of time with many Rapo players, sometimes even weeks before she revealed herself or I got my head out of my ass. Let's not forget cock teasers. I'd guess there were at least five, one in particular, Jennifer, is still on my mind. My God! What a bod! Hugh Hefner would get down and beg.

Many only spent a night, some came back once or twice more. They were only curious, not interested in an affair after all. At least twenty could not bring themselves to enter Phase Two after months of courtship, several pseudo and real dates. There were three gold diggers, the longest lasted four weeks. None of these were really affairs but they ended all the same.

WHAT HAPPENS?

It ends when guilt overwhelms her, when her erratic behavior overwhelms you, when your erratic behavior overwhelms her, when her immaturity drives you crazy, when your lack of immaturity drives her crazy, when she meets Mr. Rite, when you meet Ms.

Rite, when her boyfriend quits her, when she meets a man she likes better, when you meet a young woman you like better.

Plus, it ends for all the same reasons it does with a woman. You know most of them but here are two examples: (1) you get bored or she does. (2) she gets possessive, wanting to know where you were, who you were with, why you can't see her this weekend.

However, when you get possessive it's erratic. You know better but the first few times you'll tend to forget the inherent impossibilities and start acting like she's your girl friend, not a delightful, fun young woman you're having an affair with. Erratic, suspect, foolish, yes but that ends it.

DICKIN' AROUND WITH NITROGLYCERIN

It makes no difference that she announced her commitment to Jimmy. And, it makes no difference that you were honest with her about the long term impossibilities. The first time you fall in love with a young woman things get crazy quickly. If she doesn't have a boyfriend or if they break up during your affair, it doesn't get crazy, it gets psychotic. But when you fall in love with her and she has an unannounced boyfriend, advanced schizophrenia infects you both. Just follow this recipe from my own kitchen.

DON'S RECIPE FOR TROUBLE

Begin with: A month's worth of lusty, hot, hard, wet sex, with her wanting and taking all you've got. During the second month add giggle-filled games of tag in the park, playful wrestling on the living room floor, clowning with silly faces, some pillow fights and laughter, lots and lots of laughter. Mix all this with pleasant, quiet love making in the afternoon, ice cream cone-walks by the sea, evenings by the fire holding hands, gentle touching and face caressing.

In the fifth week begin adding:

1 Cup Her-Guilt for lying to you and to him.

2 Cups Her-Double-Guilt for cheating on her boyfriend

with you and cheating on you with her boyfriend.

3 Cups Her-Self-Condemnation for making love with two different "men" within hours of each other.

By the eighth week dump in:

1 Gallon Her-Confusing-Sex-With-Love over multiple orgasms with you when he can't last long enough for one.

1 Gallon Your-Confusing-Sex-With-Love over how alive and masculine you feel with her.

2 Quarts Her-Disorienting-Embarrassment for thinking of you while she sucks him off once she feels too guilty to "do it" with him.

Stir well for two weeks. Suddenly add:

1 Bushel Your-Hurt-Feelings when your foolish dreams and hopes are smashed once you suspect his presence.

Blend with:

2 Bushels Your-Indignant-Rage when she lies and continues to lie.

2 Truckloads Your-Jealousy created by insecurity and lack of confidence.

3 Truckloads Your-Humiliation for the scenes you make behaving like a foolish, love struck boy. (Add this twice a week until the end.)

After every scene add:

2 Barrels Your-Promises never to do it again. (Add as necessary.)

For salty flavoring throw in:

Her Tears, Your Tears, an ocean of each. (Add as required, usually every other night until the end, then nightly for weeks.)

Slowly stir, quickly adding:

4 Barrels Her-Quadruple-Guilt for lying about lying, to you and to him.

Combine with:

2 Tons Your-Fear it's about to end, **2 Tons Her-Fear** it's about to end, **4 Tons Her-Double-Fear** she will lose you both.

Mix well for two more weeks.

Observe it comes to a rolling boil all by itself. Stand back. It's explosive.

I was blown up only once.

This recipe can be used anytime you fall in love with her. It just takes longer to reach the boiling point when her boyfriend's announced or she doesn't have one. The principle ingredients are the same, grand sex, laughter, fun, hidden motives, guilt, fear, confusion, foolish dreams, loss of touch with reality, unrealistic expectations, lies, rage, scenes, unkeepable promises, insecurity, jealousy and tears, lots of tears.

The Secret: Never use even one grain of common sense.

SAFETY PRECAUTIONS
Some explosions can be prevented. Step one is to engrave, on the inside of your foolishly proud, 1950 model, male ego:

"She has a boyfriend. I was second, I am second, I will always be second. I cannot be first. I will not try to be first. We can only have fun and enjoy life. I accept it. I don't like it, I accept it."

An explosion always ends it. There are other ways.

SHE CHANGES, THAT ENDS IT
She gets the benefit of your manliness, knowledge, power and money. She learns about the world and what makes it really work. You get the benefit of her beauty, aliveness and femaleness. You learn how to enjoy life again, how to live right here, right now. It is a good trade for you both but it cannot last across time. Three months, a year, perhaps two but longer is

just not possible, she changes so quickly.

Two years with you is the same as eight years without you. If she's 19 when you begin, by the time she's 21 she knows more about everything than any woman of 31 who married her high school boyfriend at 20 and lasted seven years. And, she knows more than 27 year olds who never married.

In five months with you she learns more about the male universe than she can with boys in five years. A 20 year old will view and understand young males better than a typical, never married 25 year old.

Her perspective on life, sex and what's morally right is changed by her relationship with you. You gently get her to look at the world differently. She loses her constricted view of what's possible.

She thinks after only a few months she's a real woman, a Cosmo Girl, capable of moving in the world of adult males and handling herself. Armed with what she's learned from you she wants to go out and explore, alone. She's tasted the forbidden fruit and wants to "eat the whole thing."

You open her eyes to *The Joy of Sex*. She discovers it's not bad, immoral or wrong. It's wonderful. She wants to make it with some boys other than Jimmy just for fun. She'll lie to you about all of it, then drop you because she feels guilty. Or, you'll figure it out and be so hurt you'll drop her.

If you survive that, a few months later she realizes men are much more fun than boys and sees them in a new light. Soon she wants to try another man to find out if they're all the same. She's not nearly as afraid of them as she used to be way back six months ago when she finally spent the night with you. She'll want to see if she can control one now that she "knows" what she's doing. Plus, with her new found power she wants to compete for men, against women, just for the pure hell of it. She will.

She'll fuck him good on the first date. If he's not controllable he'll treat her half as nice as you do, rather did, and keep her on his string. He gets everything you worked so hard developing. Jesus, does that hurt. What a pisser. If he's controllable she'll keep him and you on a string, along with Jimmy. It's the same as with boys, she'll lie about it all. But you two will be finished.

Jimmy'll find out about her new man or you and drop her. Then she'll go after Jimmy with everything she's got Or, you'll realize she's got a man and your crushed ego will make you drop her. Or, she'll feel so guilty she drops you and keeps her new man. He's more exciting and besides, he never knew about you.

When things go wrong out there in the real world she'll call and attempt to re-establish a relationship with you. It's your choice. I did once, never again. When that affair re-ended I felt like the biggest fool since Walter Mondale.

All good things must end, just as all relationships with other females before her did. The end must be accepted gracefully, or any other way, but it must be accepted.

I was dangerously suicidal when my two year affair with Carla ended. Nothing, I mean nothing in my entire life crushed me as that did. Not my father rotting away from cancer for months before my eyes. Not my divorce from my second wife I loved beyond everyone but Carla.

After horrible weeks of grieving, followed by days of expressing my fears, doubts, insecurity, and the worst, feelings of mid-life hopelessness, to a good friend, I realized this too, shall pass. It did. In three months I was right back at it again with Tina, lovely, lovely 19 year old Tina.

The ending is one of the *Disadvantages*. There are more.

*"Everything has
its disadvantages."*

Worldwise Grandma, of the author

*"Take what you want
and pay for it, sayeth God."*

Spanish Proverb

Disadvantages

At 20, she is a very early adult, very late adolescent combined in one head and one heart.

ADOLESCENT: unpleasant, confused, wild mood swings, insistent, imprudent, know it all, rude, irresponsible, easily bored, sporadic, inconsistent, indiscreet, impudent, apathetic, unfocused, restless, disorganized, reckless, obstinate, inconsiderate, scatter brained, extreme, garish, preoccupied, thoughtless, awkward.

She's three to ten years away from being a woman. Got it?

You cannot take your young lover to any company functions. That's rubbing their noses in it. Do not create enemies unnecessarily. She will do that unwittingly when you take her anywhere, especially among friends.

There is a price for having a young lover. I don't mind paying it. I don't think you will either, after you get over the shock of how your "friends" and others behave.

MEN GET HARD ON'S

Male acquaintances and friends, of all ages, judge her as a person with no principles for dating someone your age, thus consider her "fair game." They try to cut in, friend or not, seeing only a piece of meat and a piece of ass for themselves.

Some of the married guys won't make any moves on her, but will attempt sabotage, not wanting you to be happy. They don't want to admit they're unhappy or don't have the balls to get divorced and do what you're doing, living life, enjoying the beauty of youth.

The husband of a woman friend and I were playing backgammon in a bar. I was working on a young cocktail waitress. As the evening wore on she agreed to have a drink with me when she got off. Five minutes after she joined us he began trying to embarrass me with snide remarks about dating girls half my age, exaggerated stories of my behavior under the influence, all in the pretext of humor. We had a loud talk in the men's room.

Divorced guys will one-up you with talk of money, their job titles, their trip to Paris, and so on, then try to move in, hoping that's how you got her to date you. When she shuts them down, they'll make an effort to destroy your relationship. It's always the envious ones, the ones who are fat, wearing polyester, with no chance to date anyone under 40 unless they buy her. They don't want to put in the effort and time needed to become an attractive man. Believe me, they're trying to ruin everything, even when it appears innocent.

WOMEN GET HOSTILE

I've been living with, married to, or dating young women for 16 years. As my long term female friends near 30, they make catty remarks or get downright hostile to my young date or current lover. These are people I've counted as loyal, trustworthy, dependable friends since 1970. They go back to being perfectly normal when I'm alone. I've had to call them all on it, after the fact of course.

Not one of them realized she was being so cuntly. They were stunned, embarrassed and apologized profusely. Christ, even a 24 year old friend of five years, behaved like an alley cat toward an 18 year old date. Phisssst, hissss! Ree-ooow!

TAKE WHAT YOU WANT AND PAY FOR IT

All you need to know is other men don't want you to succeed, especially if they are married or living with someone. Friendship? Loyalty? Don't count on that stopping any of your older male friends. They want to fuck her in the ass. Further, you only need to know every female's envious and jealous of your young lover, starting with the ex-wife and ending with your secretary.

If you prefer kissing your young lover's pink, erect nipples to sucking limp, 38 year old, brown ones, just to get one half way up, accept what your ex says. You're neurotic, trying to prove your masculinity to yourself and the world.

If you prefer your young lover who comes after only a few intense minutes of clit kissing to a woman who only begins to get wet after ten minutes of everything you can dream up, live with your friends telling you to grow up and act your age.

If you prefer holding hands with your young lover, sitting in front of the fireplace to sitting in the kitchen while a 37 year old divorcee rags on and on about what a shit her supervisor is, suck it up and survive the gossip about you.

If you prefer watching your young lover's flat, smooth stomach tense while driving it home, to looking at a flabby, stretch-marked belly wobble while you try to stay hard, tolerate society's judgement of you as a Middle Aged Crazy.

If you prefer, as I do, to watch football all day Sunday while your young lover "does her thing" somewhere else, to a Sunday outing with a divorced mother and her two children, yield to "their" wisdom. Your priorities are all screwed up.

If you prefer being accepted and respected for who and what you are by your young lover, to being ridiculed and put down by "successful" 40 year old women who compare themselves to you, power through and accept it. You're a "failure."

Then again, you could confront them all and say "I happen to like energetic, optimistic, non-ball busting females with sparkling eyes, shiny hair, smooth clear skin, strong hands and arms, well kept nails, perky tits, flat stomachs, tight vaginas, firm asses, who enjoy me and appreciate me, who don't try to own me, and on and on and on, and on."

I wouldn't advise it unless you'd enjoy looking over your shoulder for the next few years. Don't mess with the carefully constructed self images and pseudo self esteems of others. It's not important they understand you. There are disadvantages to everything. Make your choice, and live with it. Let them "live" with the choice they've made.

OTHER DISADVANTAGES

There is no long term tranquility. Her life is full of major "life-or-death" situations. Most of them are caused by her lack of experience, thus ability to solve everyday, life problems like a car that won't start, a back-stabbing co-worker, a manipulative brother, an incorrect phone bill or a period that's two days late.

Any one of these throws her whole life, and your affair, into a turmoil for three or four days. When two happen within 24 hours, she reacts like you would if the Division Manager announces your company's moving to Dumbfuck, Nebraska. A fight with her roommate over whose turn it is to clean the bathroom is as disrupting to her as a tentative diagnosis of colon cancer is to you.

Her 6'6", 235 pound boyfriend may break your face when he finds out. You've heard how she'll drop you like a rock for Mr. Rite or to reduce Shitly's sperm count to zero when he "apologizes" with tears. Don't forget it.

The green eyed monster lives in the hearts of youth. Get used to it. She wants you to display jealousy. To her, it means you genuinely care for her and are serious about the affair. Once in awhile I put on a show if words don't convince her. Once it wasn't a show. I felt jealous rage and behaved like a fool. I didn't whip up "Don's Recipe For Trouble" out of thin air, you know.

Feast or famine is reality when limiting yourself to

young women. There are times I can't get a date for weeks on end, and there are weeks my dick hurts from so much grand sex. Explanation? None, save their whimsical, unpredictable natures.

Now and then you'll feel like you are the dumbest ass on the planet. It happens when you realize she's a gold digger, a penis collector or just a tourist looking at the curious older man. I've met these types and never realized it until a month into the relationship. Not that I mind being a sex object you understand, it's just that I feel so damned stupid I didn't know it from the beginning.

You've read this several times before but I'm going to tell you again. Across time she changes and expects too much. Time changes her. Experience changes her. Knowledge changes her. Money changes her. You change her. It can't be helped but it's the biggest disadvantage.

Okay, it's time to go. A few more pages and you're outta here, Jack. On your way to lose that gut, make young friends, change everything and start living, 'cause you're gonna get old, then die.

*"Who among us
is smart enough to learn
from the mistakes of others?"*

Voltaire

*"Doing the same thing
over and over, expecting
different results,
is the definition of crazy."*

Unknown Wise Person

Closing Advice

When I got divorced single male and female friends from 19 to 45 tried to help as I attempted to date young women. The most they could do was give an opinion on what I had done wrong, time after time. They didn't have any sure-fire methods, neither do I.

My mistakes and what I've learned from them are here for you to learn from. What were my biggest? Number one: trying to date young women before I was ready. Number two: wanting the impossible from them. Number three: being too straightforward. Number four: being too nice. Number five: not understanding the difference between a married sport fuck and a potential husband.

If you quickly adopt the philosophy I eventually adopted, everything will be far less painful: "I will learn from my mistakes." I know two you'll make. In the beginning you'll be so hot to date a young woman you will come on too strong and scare her or be so accommodating it will disgust her.

After you ruin it, think about it, when you're done whipping yourself of course. Look the situation over from her vantage point. Replay everything from the beginning, include the final scene. Think, think, think. "How did she perceive that? What could I have done instead of what I did?"

It took three years after my divorce for me to become adept at meeting and dating young women. Don't expect to be going out with the Playmate of the Month because you have a how-to book. A few years from now, after three young lovers, you will easily meet, talk with and date young women.

It's necessary to fail. Like learning to ski, falling down teaches you what won't work. Accept it. You're gonna to blow it time and time again. That's necessary when learning any new skill and believe me, making yourself interesting and attractive to younger women is a skill.

Learning takes time and patience. All projects have a wheel spinning phase at the beginning. When you have nothing to show for months of effort except an empty wallet and a neck full of frustration, keep in mind that's normal. Don't quit, at least don't quit for long.

I gave up often, once for three months. Thinking back, I realize I had to quit when I did. I was doing the same things over and over, expecting different results. Just like the quote above, crazy. But I always tried again because I believed, and still do, they are the best females on the planet. Having a young lover is exhilarating, not easy.

IT'S WORTH IT AND SO IS SHE

Nothing is better than spending a long evening making love with a young woman you care deeply for, waking up with her, making love again, arriving at the office, walking across the parking lot with a full heart and an empty scrotum. Nothing in my life has felt better or been more fulfilling. Nothing.

My fondest memories are, and always shall be, of the wonderful, soft, life-filled matchless days and endless nights with my darling Carla. It was worth every tear, every heart ripping lie.

I'LL HAVE MY MEMORIES

Way back there on page one I talked about my memory getting triggered by a large breasted, black attendant at the Golden Years Retirement Villa. When that happens, I hope there's no stopping old memories from flooding my awareness.

After smiling and drooling over Genette I want to cry bittersweet, old man's tears remembering the happiest afternoon of my life. It was simple, yet miraculous.

By the sea, watching the sun go down, man and young woman. We didn't speak, didn't touch, didn't kiss, didn't even look at each other, just sat there, part of the universe. Happiness swelled within me. I became uncomfortable, not recognizing the emotion. It grew, became undeniable. I softened, allowed life and joy to overcome me. Alive! Me! I was alive, truly alive. A living, breathing, happy human being, genuinely, perfectly happy. Not pleased, not satisfied, not content. Happy, simply happy.

After a few minutes I could say, "Carla, God, I'm so happy." She smiled and took my hand.

Christ, in 30 years I hope I can still feel, like I can now, her lips pressed against my hand in tender reassurance when she noticed tears trickling from my eyes, as I watched our earth's sun, slip sadly away.

It was worth everything to have that moment with her. To know, to understand, to accept, to feel what it's really like to be alive. Never before, yet I hope someday again, to feel happiness that complete. I know now, it is possible.

"Oh, those were the days, my friend. We thought they'd never end. We'd sing and dance . . ."

They do end, unfortunately. They begin anew, if you don't quit.

PARTING SUMMARY

You won't have an affair with very many, at least not percentage-wise, just like women. Some will like you but you won't like them, and vice versa, just like women. You'll fall in love and once or twice your love will be returned, for a time, just like women. Overall it's not much different, just far, far, far more exciting, exacerbating, exhilarating, exhausting, expensive, explosive and yes, far more exquisite.

During your affair she can, and will, change direction dramatically in less than two week's time. You will be the innocent bystander struck by her careening truck of life. Always keep your circle of young friends intact. When the tire tracks across your chest have disappeared you can start again.

Young women are sent by the gods to test you yes, but to keep you humble as well. When you end up sitting across from Dream Coed at that wedding reception dinner, try to remember, "It's just a game." Even Jerry West, the greatest clutch player of all time, missed a few when it was all on the line.

You have to be the aggressor. She will not come to you. You have to get out there and find her, meet her and talk with her. It's all up to you, everything. Don't forget what Lombardi said, *"There's no such thing as luck, only preparation meeting opportunity."*

Good "luck."

R. Don Steele
Whittier, California, February, 1987.

Write and make comments, point out mistakes I've made, send me anything you'd like, or ask questions. Write to:

Steel Balls Press
Box 807
Whittier, CA 90608

Dear Reader,

My book has been out since '87. At the end of it, I offer to answer letters with questions. So many men wanted more, that I now conduct seminars and offer consulting: in-person $50 hour; by phone $30 half hour.

In my seminar, you learn powerful, advanced skills. Learning is immediate because the feedback, good old feedback, is immediate. By interacting directly with me and four young women, you quickly master two topics that are beyond the written word: courtship body language and tasteful dressing. You learn even more listening to answers and demonstrations the girls and I give to "what if" scenarios and questions from the other guys.

Additionally, Kimberly conducts *Looking Good* all day shopping tours for men. She dresses you with the taste, style and color needed to attract young women. You must have attended a seminar where the fundamentals are covered and have a wardrobe budget of $500 to $1000. Fee: $150.

I'm in the final stages of **The Young Woman's Guide To Office Politics**, guaranteed to be the perfect conversation starter. Pre-publication offer goes out late '92. Like my sense of humor in *HTD-YW?* You'll love **The Stupid Gazette**, it's my 10 year collection of articles. It will have you and your young woman rolling on the floor: failed suicides, stupid crooks, drunk drug agents, bumbling bureaucrats, porkers, do-gooders et al: 1100 articles, 330 pages, $19.95 pp. Coming soon, videos of seminars and body language.

Write me for more info on any of this. Thanks.

R. Don Steele   September 1992

p.s. Only previous buyers: additional copies of HTDYW are just $11 postage paid. Great gifts! Good only directly from Steel Balls Press.

ADVANCED SKILLS SEMINAR
Over the past six years many guys who requested in-person counseling just needed more *Looking Good* and *Courtship* info. At the seminar you learn that, and much more: Personal-

ized, constructive advice from four young women, plus six hours of my expertise.

ADVANTAGES

You save months, even years, of frustration learning these skills here, not thru trial and error.

You learn directly from young women who are honest and blunt, but respectful.

You get personalized information applicable to your own situation and needs.

You learn in a controlled, safe atmosphere, where nobody is ever embarrassed or ridiculed.

You learn by doing, then getting feedback, the only way to master these crucial skills.

You learn about any topic you choose during the Open Forum part of the day.

You talk with me individually many times during the day to pick my brain on any subject.

You learn during the coming months reviewing your audio or video tape of the seminar.

Dress For Success With Young Women

Kimberly explains the style of dress needed to attract young women. Each guy can bring four outfits: Office, College Class, Tennis Date and Casual Party. The girls give you private feedback, suggesting ways to increase your appeal.

Julee, my stylist, is there to privately discuss your hair and suggest a cut that improves your attractiveness.

Courtship Body Language

Knowing which young woman is interested in you is the key to being successful. The young women demonstrate what to look for and how to verify her interest so you don't get shot down approaching the wrong one.

The girls help me show you how a young woman communicates her interest in you *from across the room* by using posture shifts, the direction she faces, the type of smile, how she breaks off eye contact and many other subtle signals.

Then they show you how she communicates even more subtly *when talking with you*. Learn the enormous significance of how she touches herself or objects, the way she sits or stands plus many other gestures. Know when to back off, when to move ahead, and when to bide your time.

Conversation Openers

I demonstrate techniques to get her attention in a class-room, at a party, or at the office. The young women show you methods to start up a conversation that grabs her interest.

Pick Your Seat

Cathy and Syndee demonstrate and explain the how's and why's of carefully choosing where you sit in the office cafeteria, classroom or club meeting. It's crucial: don't alarm her, don't let her know you're strongly interested, but do make her comfortable talking with you.

WHAT TO BRING

The most important thing you bring to the seminar is *The Right Attitude*, not the one I describe on page 76, but rather a commitment to learn by doing, plus a dedication to learn from *good old feedback* as I describe it on page 82.

The second most important thing to bring is your copy of *HTDYW* with pages marked where you want more information. During the breaks, show these to me and I'll give you the answers, ideas, or explanations, one on one.

Remember, nothing is mandatory, everything is voluntary. Other things you should bring are listed below. It's not required, but I recommend a video camera so that you can record my lengthy demonstration with the girls on courtship body language.

DRESS FOR SUCCESS WITH YOUNG WOMEN

Wear suit/tie or jacket/tie you wear to work; bring two other ties. Bring these outfits: Casual party at a friend's house where young women will be; Tennis/racquetball date with a young woman; College class, everyone is under 30 except you. (Outfit means everything from head to toe.)

Bring all of your distance, reading and sunglasses. Wear the cologne you think young women like. Bring it and your other bottles of cologne.

TALKING WITH YOUNG WOMEN

Bring at least two magazines young women read. Mark articles, including some on celebrities you can use as conversational material with my young assistants.

Bring several tapes/cds of artists young women like. From the newspaper, bring ads for concerts you'd attend with a young woman.

Bring a list of your favorite ten movies and your favorite female celebrities.

Bring your business card per page 64.

Bring a book of paper matches, deck of playing cards, and three dimes and three pennies.

Bring, committed to memory, two-minute autobiography per page 157 you can use in conversation with a young assistant. (If you're just starting out it can be one-page written.)

Bring, committed to memory, your answers to *Her Inevitable Questions* that begin on page 150. (If you're just starting out, you may have crib notes.) The girls will pop these questions on you at the most unexpected times during the day.

UNDERSTANDING YOUNG WOMEN

In an unmarked envelope, put five questions that you want answered frankly and to the point. Give these to me when you arrive. I pop them on the girls throughout the day. Concentrate on topics only a *young* woman knows the answers to.

ENROLLING

Many men are concerned they might be embarrassed. Not to worry, everything is voluntary, besides that, we're all friendly, kind and respectful.

Seminars are Sundays from 10 to 4. Write and find out when the next one is. Then, send the application and $95. I'll send directions to the seminar location. If you're flying in and staying overnight, request the 800 number of a nearby, recommended motel and directions from LAX.

Please be prompt. Doors open at 9:45 am. Coffee/rolls are provided. Box lunches are available from Lascari's for $7, or bring your own. We do a working lunch.

SEMINAR APPLICATION

Name _____ Age _____

Address _____

City _____ Zip_____

Height _____ Weight _____ Education _____

Youngest Successfully Dated Since Divorce _____

REVIEWERS AGREE

Steele is hardheadedly practical. He's worked out as sure-fire a method as you'll find for bridging the sexual-generation gap. *Michael Perkins, Screw Magazine*

Steele pulls no punches as he explains how to attract the young, from dress codes to actions. The honest approaches and advice are unusually solid and explicit. Everything from sex and the young woman to analyses of her value system and psyche with step-by-step courting scenarios, placing emphasis on strategy based on understanding. Men interested in a no-holds-barred approach will find this one of the most refreshing guides available. Women not involved in defining chauvinist behavior will learn a lot, too. *Diane Donovan, Chicago Tribune*

Gloves off truth! Far more than a dating book. Bold, harsh, funny, human, an unpredictable page-turner. A must read for divorced men. *Edward Haldeman, Single Fathers United*

Steele's unique style is nearly conversational, one of his strongest points as a writer. It makes for easy reading and creates and atmosphere totally lacking of preaching. His method of illustrating key points by telling actual stories of his own missteps and his successes makes for an interesting and engaging way to learn. *John E. Dempsey, Divorced Men's Council, Southern California*

Solid advice presented in an entertaining, sometimes hilarious, sometimes touching manner. Read this book! *Kirk Matthews, Denver Singles Alliance*

Other books for men give pep talks and sure-fire opening lines. Steele cuts through that crap. His methods of setting up cross-routines with young women you are interested in will work with women of any age. Just this detailed advice is worth the price of the book. *Ron Macdonald, Single Scene, USA's largest singles newspaper*